PreK–12 English Language Proficiency Standards

Augmentation of the World-Class Instructional Design and Assessment (WIDA) Consortium English Language Proficiency Standards

TESOL   **Teachers of English to Speakers of Other Languages, Inc.**

Typeset in Berkeley and News Gothic
by Capitol Communication Systems, Inc., Crofton, Maryland USA
Printed by: United Graphics Incorporated, Mattoon, Illinois USA

Teachers of English to Speakers of Other Languages, Inc.
700 South Washington Street, Suite 200
Alexandria, Virginia 22314 USA
Tel 703-836-0774 • Fax 703-836-6447 • E-mail tesol@tesol.org • http://www.tesol.org/

PreK–12 English Language Proficiency Standards Team:
    Margo Gottlieb, World-Class Instructional Design and Assessment (WIDA)
        Consortium and Illinois Resource Center
    Lynore Carnuccio, ESL-Etc Educational Consultants
    Gisela Ernst-Slavit, Washington State University
    Anne Katz, School for International Training
    With contributions from Marguerite Ann Snow, Cal State Los Angeles

Publishing Manager: Carol Edwards
Copy Editors: Kelly Graham and Ellen Garshick
Cover Design: Amanda Van Staalduinen
Text Graphics and Photography: Tomiko Chapman

ISBN 978-1-931185-31-8
Library of Congress Control No. 2006903709

Contents

List of Figures

Preface

Over the past decade, thousands upon thousands of English language learners with diverse languages, cultures, and educational experiences have entered our schools and professional lives. During the same period, pedagogy has changed and accountability has clamped down on our school districts. As teachers, we recognize the linguistic and cultural richness of our classrooms. At the same time, we realize the importance of providing our students access to rigorous, standards-based assessment, curriculum, and instruction as they gain English language proficiency.

PreK–12 English Language Proficiency Standards offers an up-to-date resource for *each and every* educator who works with English language learners in today's classrooms, irrespective of the number of students or the type of instructional model.

This revised edition of TESOL's (1997) *ESL Standards for PreK–12 Students* draws on current theory, sound classroom practice, and educational standards from an array of national organizations and states. Its focus is on English language learners' oral language and literacy development through academic content. At the same time, it recognizes the importance of the students' native languages and cultures, the social and sociocultural dimensions of language acquisition, and the intercultural and cross-cultural connections among languages, peoples, and societies.

The acquisition of English is a complex undertaking at any age. The heterogeneity of the student population and its range of performance are tremendous. As teachers of English language learners, we are responsible for targeting how individual students use language, the context of that interaction, and the types of support that facilitate meaningful communication. The English language proficiency standards help delineate that process.

Above all else, *PreK–12 English Language Proficiency Standards* is meant for sharing among educators who work with English language learners. To encourage collaboration, we emphasize that, although the standards are intended to remain constant, their elements are variable, flexible, and dynamic. Teachers and administrators are welcome and encouraged to adopt, adapt, or apply the contents through ongoing conversations, learning communities, or sustained professional development.

TESOL is an international advocate for the profession. We applaud the foresight and insight of the organization in creating, supporting, and updating its content standards for elementary and secondary students for whom English is an additional language. With the 2006 publication of this volume, TESOL remains at the forefront of standards-based reform for educators of second language learners.

It is our sincere hope that this volume offers you ideas for renewed, rich, and rewarding educational experiences with English language learners.

The PreK–12 English Language Proficiency Standards Team
Margo Gottlieb, Chair
Lynore M. Carnuccio
Gisela Ernst-Slavit
Anne Katz

Overview

PreK–12
English Language
Proficiency Standards

Standard 1: English language learners **communicate** for **social, intercultural,** and **instructional** purposes within the school setting

Standard 2: English language learners **communicate** information, ideas, and concepts necessary for academic success in the area of **language arts**

Standard 3: English language learners **communicate** information, ideas, and concepts necessary for academic success in the area of **mathematics**

Standard 4: English language learners **communicate** information, ideas, and concepts necessary for academic success in the area of **science**

Standard 5: English language learners **communicate** information, ideas, and concepts necessary for academic success in the area of **social studies**

Overview

This volume is a revision of *ESL Standards for Pre-K–12 Students* (TESOL, 1997). This section states the rationale for revising the standards, illustrates the relationship between the two sets of standards, identifies potential audiences and uses, and outlines the contents of this book.

Rationale for Revision

In the nearly 10 years since the publication of TESOL's ESL standards, the standards movement has continued to grow and affect educational systems throughout the country at the state, district, and classroom levels. Standards remain the engine for educational reform that seeks to ensure that all students, including English language learners, have access to high-quality instruction by defining the range of competence within academic content areas, providing a clear and consistent basis for assessment, and serving as the basis for accountability systems.

With the increasing emphasis on academic achievement has come a growing recognition that content-based instruction and assessment provide better access for English language learners to the general education curriculum and that students need to develop academic language proficiency in order to negotiate that curriculum. More than ever, the educational community recognizes the urgency of ensuring that English language learners have access to a full range of opportunities within the school setting, including the arts (e.g., music, fine arts), internships, clubs, Advanced Placement courses, special education support services, sports teams, gifted and talented programs, and community service. Language provides the infrastructure for success in all facets of school, including extracurricular and academic pursuits.

Thus, in addition to the language proficiency needed for social, intercultural, and instructional purposes, the new TESOL standards target academic language proficiency in four core content areas: language arts, mathematics, science, and social studies.

The focus on academic language is supported by research on effective second language (L2) instruction as well as by the provisions of the No Child Left Behind Act of 2001. To meet the language needs of English language learners, each state must develop English language proficiency standards grounded in state academic content standards and encompassing the language domains of listening, speaking, reading, and writing. This volume provides an up-to-date resource for teachers, administrators, and teacher educators involved in the education of English language learners and a model for states and districts working to meet federal guidelines.

The goals from TESOL's 1997 volume have been reconfigured in the new English language proficiency standards. Figure 1 shows a generalized view of the relationship between the two sets of standards. Goals 1 and 3 have been integrated into Standard 1, and Goal 2 has expanded to shape Standards 2–5.

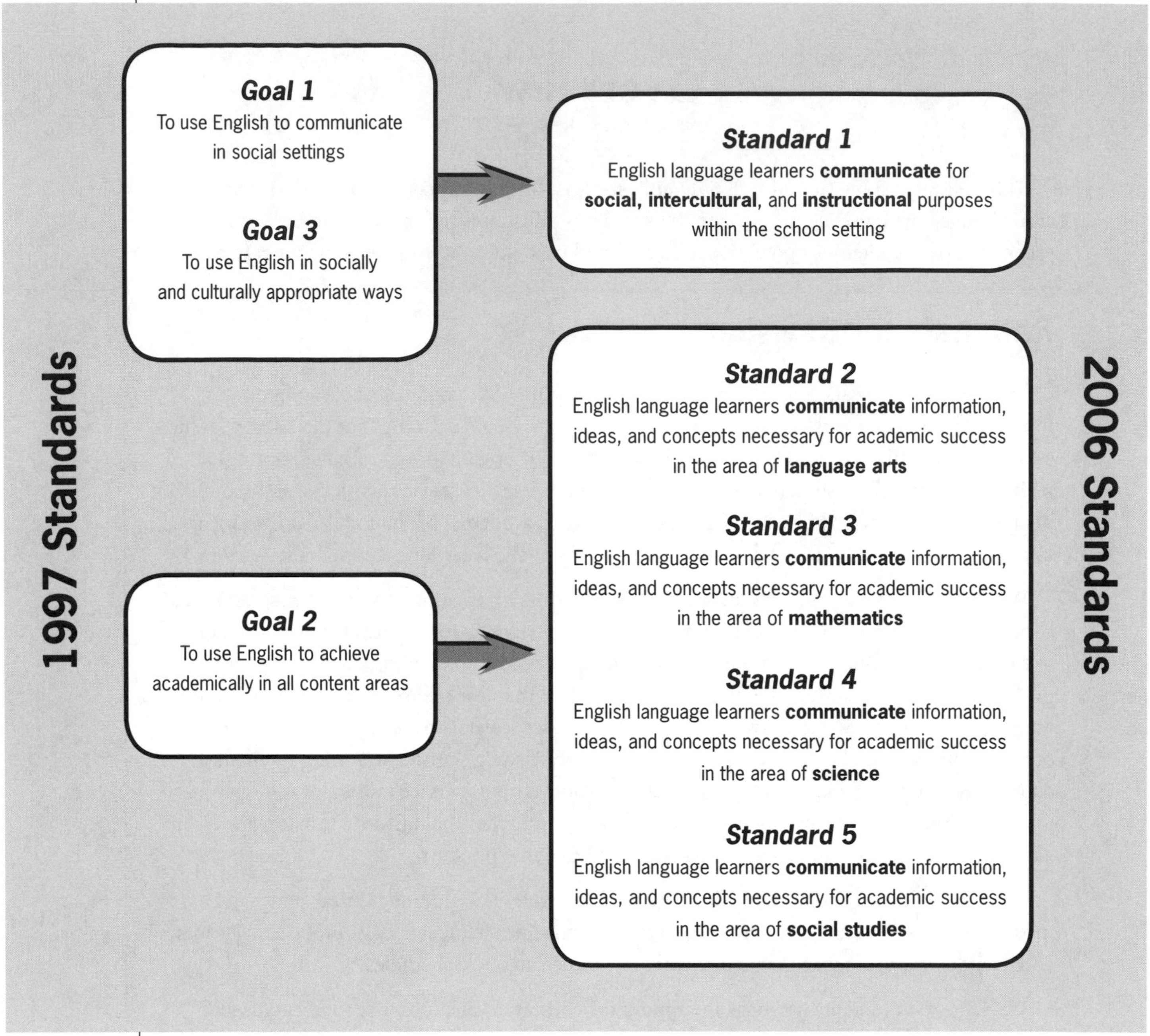
1997 Standards
Goal 1
To use English to communicate in social settings
Goal 3
To use English in socially and culturally appropriate ways
Goal 2
To use English to achieve academically in all content areas
2006 Standards
Standard 1
English language learners communicate for social, intercultural, and instructional purposes within the school setting
Standard 2
English language learners communicate information, ideas, and concepts necessary for academic success in the area of language arts
Standard 3
English language learners communicate information, ideas, and concepts necessary for academic success in the area of mathematics
Standard 4
English language learners communicate information, ideas, and concepts necessary for academic success in the area of science
Standard 5
English language learners communicate information, ideas, and concepts necessary for academic success in the area of social studies

Figure 1. Relationship Between TESOL's Two Sets of PreK–12 Standards

Audiences and Potential Uses

The English language proficiency standards are useful for all educators working with English language learners in preK–12 settings. Depending on how states, districts, and schools configure the delivery of instruction to English language learners, those educators may include ESL teachers, bilingual teachers, content teachers, resource staff, special education teachers, administrators, and mainstream teachers.

This volume is intended for educators who design, provide, and oversee instruction and assessment for English language learners. The focus is on a standards-driven classroom where instruction and performance assessment are intertwined. No matter who works with English language learners, students are to be actively engaged in learning, have ample opportunities for interaction, and demonstrate their English language proficiency in multiple and varied ways.

A variety of potential uses for the standards are outlined in Figure 2, alongside the primary stakeholder or audience. The education community works with or serves English language learners in many capacities, and this volume can readily be used as an advocacy tool on their behalf.

Audience	Potential Uses
ESL, bilingual, and dual-language teachers	Help develop language objectives and lesson plans
	Monitor progress of English language teachers
	Collaborate and network with other teachers
	Coordinate native and second language support services
Content teachers (e.g., for sheltered instruction or specially designed academic instruction in English)	Help develop language and content objectives and lesson plans
	Align English language proficiency standards with academic content standards
	Reinforce language development of English language learners
General education or mainstream classroom teachers	Differentiate instruction of English language learners by language proficiency level
	Collaborate with ESL, bilingual, and content teachers
	Offer a common referent for communication
Special education teachers	Design language goals for individualized education plans (IEPs)
	Glean ideas on expected performance of English language learners
	Document students' movement through the stages of second language acquisition
Program administrators	Revisit program design and allocation of teacher assignments
	Align and augment state English language proficiency standards
	Anchor or benchmark student samples
School and district administrators	Contextualize state assessment data
	Observe teachers and classes
	Provide targets for school and district improvement plans
	Plan community outreach

Figure 2. Audiences and Potential Uses of the English Language Proficiency Standards

Audience	Potential Uses
Curriculum coordinators	Map standards onto curriculum
	Align and augment curriculum
	Develop thematic units and model lessons
	Align with resource materials and student samples
Teacher educators	Infuse into undergraduate and graduate course work
	Incorporate into field experiences (e.g., student teaching practicum)
	Integrate into final or research projects
	Sensitize other teacher educators to the needs of English language learners
Educational consultants	Incorporate into professional development activities (e.g., instructional assessment strategies)
	Provide technical assistance on standards-based education
	Advocate on behalf of English language learners and their families
Test developers and test users	Ground classroom assessment
	Develop reliable and valid measures
	Create task and test specifications
	Analyze and report standards-referenced data
Researchers and evaluators	Study impact (washback) on implementation at the district, school, and classroom levels or as case studies of teachers
	Validate the second language development process
	Determine relationship between standards, instruction, and assessment
	Analyze strengths and challenges of support services for English language learerss

Figure 2 (continued). Audiences and Potential Uses of the English Language Proficiency Standards

Features and Content

Using TESOL's (1997) *ESL Standards for Pre-K–12 Students* as a foundation, the preK–12 English language proficiency standards

- expand the scope and breadth of the ESL content standards by connecting them to specific core curriculum content areas, namely, English language arts, mathematics, science, and social studies

- value students' native languages[1] and cultures as the foundation for developing academic language proficiency

- acknowledge the social and intercultural aspects of language development

- provide an organizational structure that is synchronized with U.S. federal legislation

The English language proficiency standards also draw on other standards-based frameworks relevant to the instructional goals English language learners must meet in U.S. schools. They build on the World-Class Instructional Design and Assessment (WIDA) Consortium's[2] (2004) *English Language Proficiency Standards for English Language Learners in Kindergarten Through Grade 12* and on a review of national and state content standards in English language arts, mathematics, science, and social studies. (For a list of state standards and curriculum documents, see Source Documents and References for Further Reading.)

The following features frame the preK–12 English language proficiency standards:

- a conceptual framework for standards-based classroom instruction and assessment

- consolidation of the existing ESL standards and addition of new standards with strands of sample performance indicators devoted to the language of the core curriculum areas

- reorganization of the standards and sample progress indicators according to language domain (listening, speaking, reading, writing) and level of language proficiency

- reconfiguration of the grade-level clusters (preK–K, 1–3, 4–5, 6–8, and 9–12)

- suggestions for applying the English language proficiency standards

- topics derived from standards of national professional organizations and states

- updated references, resources, and glossary

- frequently asked questions about the English language proficiency standards (see Appendix A)

---

[1]*Native language* and *first language* are used throughout to indicate students' primary or home language.

[2]The WIDA Consortium is a group of multiple states, formed in 2002 with federal monies, that, among its projects, has developed comprehensive English language proficiency standards and assessment.

Conceptual Framework

Conceptual Framework

This section outlines the backdrop for the development of standards for English language learners of the 21st century. The English language proficiency standards build on the theoretical framework established by TESOL's (1997) *ESL Standards for Pre-K–12 Students*. Two sections from that volume follow: TESOL's Vision of Effective Education for All Students (with certain terminology changed to reflect current usage) and General Principles of Language Acquisition. This foundational work is extended in a model that considers the complex factors influencing language development in schools and uses the model to focus on relevant aspects of language in designing instruction and assessment.

TESOL's Vision of Effective Education for All Students

The role of English language proficiency standards can only be fully understood within the broader context of education for English language learners. Therefore, before presenting the English language proficiency standards, we describe TESOL's overarching vision of effective education.

- Effective education for English language learners includes advanced or nativelike levels of proficiency in English.

- Effective education for English language learners includes the maintenance and promotion of students' native languages in school and community contexts.

- All education personnel assume responsibility for the education of English language learners.

- Effective education also calls for the comprehensive provision of high-quality services and full access to those services by all students.

- Knowledge of more than one language and culture is advantageous for all students.

Effective education for English language learners includes advanced or nativelike levels of proficiency in English

For English language learners to be successful in school and ultimately in the world outside school, they must be able to use English to accomplish their academic, personal, and social goals with the same proficiency as native speakers of English. In school environments, English language learners need to be able to use spoken and written English both to acquire academic content and to demonstrate their learning. They also need to be able to follow routine classroom instructions given in English and understand and use appropriate communication patterns so that they can be successful learners in academic environments. Finally, English language learners need to use English to function effectively in social settings outside the school as well as in academic settings. The English language proficiency standards in this volume are concerned with these types of social and academic skills. Moreover, appropriate performance and assessment standards that distinguish between language and academic achievement are also required if English language learners are to be given full credit for learning academic content while acquiring English.

Effective education for English language learners includes the maintenance and promotion of students' native languages in school and community contexts

By definition, English language learners already know and use another language. Both the academic achievement and the school completion of English language learners are significantly enhanced when these learners are able to use their native languages to learn in school. In fact, full proficiency in the native language (including literacy) facilitates second language development. Developing and using English language learners' native languages also serves U.S. national interests because it increases the linguistic and cultural resources available as the United States participates in a global society. Bilingualism is an asset whose value for the individual and for society can only increase as the U.S. role in the global marketplace continues to expand in this century.

All education personnel assume responsibility for the education of English language learners

The attainment of challenging, world-class educational standards by all students is possible only if schools design their educational missions with English language learners, as well as others, in mind. Comprehensive education calls for shared responsibility and collaboration among all educational professionals working with English language learners. It also calls for professionals to expand their knowledge to encompass issues of relevance to the education of English language learners. This expanded knowledge base includes an understanding of the similarities and differences in first and second language acquisition; the role of the native language in second language and content learning; instructional methods and strategies that facilitate both English language and content learning; instructional practices that accommodate individual differences in learning styles; the interrelationships among culture, cognition, and academic achievement; alternative approaches to assessment; and the importance of community-school linkages in education. These are all part of the professional development of ESL specialists that general educators must tap into if educational reform is to result in the attainment of high standards by all students.

In addition, the accountability demands of the past decade make it even more critical that all teachers who serve English language learners work together with shared understanding and mutual goals for their students.

Effective education also calls for the comprehensive provision of high-quality services and full access to those services by all students

High-quality educational experiences and services must be fully accessible to all English language learners. These experiences and services include, among others, comprehensive and challenging curricula, access to the full range of curricula (e.g., gifted classes, special education services, laboratory sciences, college preparatory courses), safe and well-equipped classrooms, appropriate instructional practices and assessment measures, inclusion in extracurricular activities, and fully and appropriately certified teachers and other educational specialists and resources. However, this is often not the case in many schools. To have high-quality programs and to serve English language learners appropriately on their way to mastery of English, instruction must take into account the varying entry-level English abilities of English language learners. Some learners come to school with oral and written skills; others do not. In addition, when possible, programs should provide some instruction in the native languages of English language learners. TESOL's *Access Brochure* (see TESOL, 1997, Appendix A) provides a description of the conditions needed to provide English language learners with equitable opportunities to learn.

Knowledge of more than one language and culture is advantageous for all students

Internationalism is the hallmark of modern U.S. education and of the education reform movement, and linguistic and cultural diversity are the hallmarks of internationalism. The challenge of contemporary education is to contribute to students' abilities to live in increasingly diverse local communities and an ever-shrinking world community. Effective education for the 21st century must provide firsthand opportunities for students to learn about the cultural diversity around them and to learn world languages. Cross-cultural competence can be fostered by meaningful and long-term interactions with others with different world views, life experiences, languages, and cultures. Language learning can be fostered by interactions with native English speakers. This means that not only should English language learners learn about the United States from native English speakers, but native-English-speaking students, teachers, administrators, and school staff should learn about the world and its languages from English language learners, their families, and their communities.

General Principles of Language Acquisition

A number of general principles derived from research and theory about the nature of language, language learning, human development, and pedagogy underlie the English language proficiency standards described in this volume. These principles are described briefly here.

- Language is functional.

- Language varies.

- Language learning is cultural learning.

- Language acquisition is a long-term process.

- Language acquisition occurs through meaningful interaction and challenging content.

- Language processes develop interdependently.

- Native language proficiency contributes to second language acquisition.

- Bilingualism is an individual and societal asset.

Language is functional

Language, oral and written, is primarily a means of communication used by people in multiple and varied social contexts to express themselves, interact with others, learn about the world, and meet their individual and collective needs. Successful language learning and language teaching emphasize the goal of functional proficiency. This is a departure from traditional pedagogical approaches that view language learning and teaching primarily as mastery of the elements of language, such as grammar and vocabulary, without reference to their functional usefulness in communication. *Thus, what is most important for English language learners is to function effectively in and through English while learning challenging academic content.*

Language varies

Language, oral and written, is not monolithic; it comes in different varieties. Language varies according to the person, topic, purpose, and situation. All people are proficient in more than one of these social varieties of their native language. Language also varies with respect to regional, social class, and ethnic-group differences. Such language varieties are characterized by distinctive lexical, structural, and functional characteristics, and they constitute legitimate and functional systems of communication within their respective sociocultural niches. Additionally, language varies from one academic domain to another—the language of mathematics is different from the language of social studies. As competent language users, English language learners already use their own language varieties. They must also learn the oral and written language varieties used in schools and in the communities at large. What is most important for English language learners is to function effectively in social and academic environments while retaining their own native language varieties.

Language learning is cultural learning

Patterns of language usage vary across cultures and reflect differences in values, norms, and beliefs about social roles and relationships in each culture. When children learn their first language, they learn the cultural values, norms, and beliefs that are characteristic of their cultures. To learn another language is to learn new norms, behaviors, and beliefs that are appropriate in the new culture, and thus to extend one's sociocultural competence to new environments. To add a new language, therefore, is to add a new culture. Learning a new language and culture also provides insights into one's own language and culture. This goal is important for English language learners because general education in U.S. schools tends to reflect a culture other than their own. If English language learners are to attain the same high standards as native-English-speaking students, educational programs must be based on acknowledgment of, understanding of, respect for, and valuing of diverse cultural backgrounds. What is important for all language learners is to develop additive bilingualism and biculturalism.

Language acquisition is a long-term process

Language acquisition occurs over time with learners moving through developmental stages and gradually growing in proficiency. Individual learners, however, move through these stages at variable rates. Rates of acquisition are influenced by multiple factors, including an individual's educational background, first language background, learning style, cognitive style, motivation, and personality. In addition, sociocultural factors, such as the influence of the English or native language community in the learner's life, may play a role in acquisition. In many instances, learners "pick up" conversation skills related to social language more quickly than they acquire academic language skills. Educational programs must recognize the length of time it takes to acquire the English language skills necessary for success in school. *Consequently, English language learners must be given the time it takes to attain full academic proficiency in English—often from 5 to 10 years.*

Language acquisition occurs through meaningful interaction and challenging content

Research in first and second language acquisition indicates that language is learned most effectively when it is used in meaningful situations as learners interact with others (some of whom should be more proficient than the learners are) to accomplish their purposes. Language acquisition takes place as learners engage in activities of a social nature with opportunities to practice language forms for a variety of communicative purposes. Language acquisition also takes place during activities that are of a cognitive or intellectual nature, where learners have opportunities to become skilled in using language for reasoning and mastery of challenging new information. *Thus, English language learners must have multiple opportunities to use English, to interact with others as they study meaningful and intellectually challenging content, and to receive feedback on their use of both oral and written language.*

Language processes develop interdependently

Distinctions among the processes of reading, listening, writing, and speaking are artificial. So is the conceptualization that language acquisition is linear (with listening preceding speaking, speaking preceding reading, and so forth). Authentic language often entails the simultaneous use of different language domains, and acquisition of functional language abilities occurs simultaneously and interdependently, rather than sequentially. Thus, for example, depending on the age of the learner, reading activities may activate the development of speaking abilities or vice versa. Additionally, listening, speaking, reading, and writing develop as learners engage with and through different modes and technologies, such as computers, music, film, and video. *Therefore, English language learners need to interact in learning environments that promote the integration of listening, speaking, reading, and writing. They also need to develop all of their language abilities through the use of varied modes and technologies.*

Native language proficiency contributes to second language acquisition

Because, by definition, English language learners know and use at least one other language, they have acquired an intuitive understanding of the general structural and functional characteristics of language. They bring this knowledge to the task of second language learning. Some English language learners also come to the task of learning English and learning content through English already literate in their native languages. These learners know what it means to be literate—they know that they can use written forms of language to learn more about the world, to convey information and receive information from others, to establish and maintain relationships with others, and to explore the perspectives of others. Literacy in the native language correlates positively with the acquisition of literacy in a second language. In addition, academic instruction that includes the use of students' native languages, especially if they are literate in that language, promotes learners' academic achievement while they are acquiring the English needed to benefit fully from instruction through English. Native language literacy abilities can assist English language learners in English-medium classrooms to construct meaning from academic materials and experiences in English. And, in learning a new language, students also learn more about their native language. *This means that, for English language learners, the most effective environments for second language teaching and learning are those that promote these learners' native languages and literacy development as a foundation for English language and academic development.*

Bilingualism is an individual and societal asset

Acquisition of two languages simultaneously is a common and normal developmental phenomenon, and acquisition of a second (or third) language can confer certain cognitive and linguistic advantages on the individual. To realize these benefits, however, an advanced level of proficiency in both languages is necessary. Therefore, the most effective educational environments for English language learners are those that promote the continued development of learners' first or native languages for both academic and social purposes. In addition, as noted earlier, bilingual proficiency enhances employment possibilities in the international marketplace and enhances the competitive strength of U.S. industry and business worldwide. *This means that bilingualism benefits the individual and serves the national interest, and schools need to promote the retention and development of multiple languages.*

Language Proficiency in School

A Model for Understanding Language Proficiency in School

To capture the complexity of language proficiency in school, the model in Figure 3 depicts the dimensions that affect the language development process. These dimensions encompass cognitive, sociocultural, and linguistic factors. The model is designed to assist educators in understanding the many layers that underpin students' language performances in the classroom. Although the dimensions are displayed as separate components, they operate interactively as students learn and use language in school.

Cognitive factors describe the processes required for learning that expand the students' knowledge base. Successful students utilize a variety of learning strategies that facilitate higher order thinking skills and draw on metalinguistic and metacognitive awareness. For example, students may provide a detailed explanation of a process, such as scientific inquiry, or the steps involved in solving a math problem. Students and teachers develop this dimension through a variety of school experiences designed to support students in increasing their knowledge base.

Sociocultural factors include a range of contextual influences that impact the teaching and learning process. Affective factors such as attitudes, motivation, investment, and resilience as well as the influences of native languages and cultures, such as the degree of literacy in the first language and family expectations, bear directly on achievement. As members of the school community, students must learn the accepted behaviors, practices, and habits of school culture, such as raising one's hand, completing homework in a timely fashion, and demonstrating respect

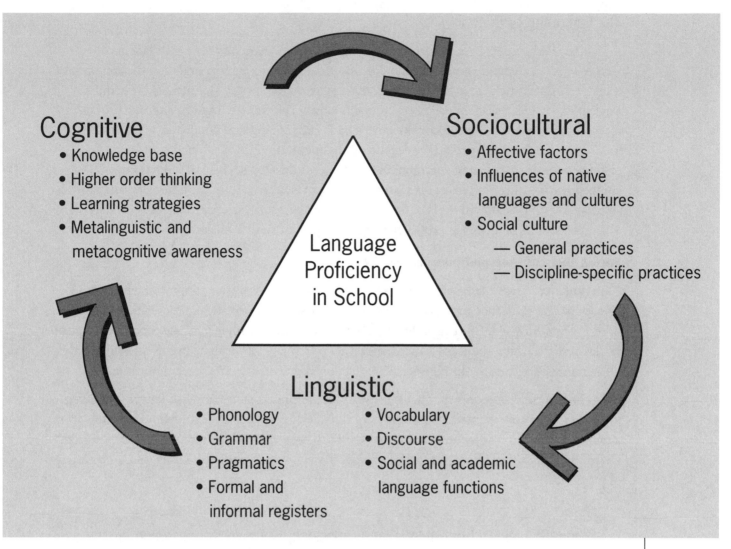

Figure 3. A Model for Understanding Language Proficiency in School: Cognitive, Sociocultural, and Linguistic Dimensions

for others. In addition, as students move across grade levels, they are expected to acculturate to the norms, values, and beliefs of the content-area disciplines. In other words, becoming members of a discipline-based discourse community entails students learning, for example, to think like scientists or write like historians.

Linguistic factors refer to the range of language features required of English language learners for successful communication in school. These features include phonology, grammar (syntax), pragmatics, and discourse. They also comprise vocabulary, social and academic language functions, and informal and formal registers.

This model provides a window on the developmental path students take as they negotiate school learning. The English language proficiency standards draw on cognitive, sociocultural, and linguistic dimensions to focus on relevant aspects of language in the design of instruction and assessment for English language learners in schools.

The Language of School

In a curriculum centered on standards, all students, and particularly English language learners, face demanding academic and cognitive requirements across content areas and grade levels. To fully participate in school, English language learners must simultaneously acquire English and achieve academically across content areas. The view of English language proficiency represented in the standards recognizes the broad range of language competencies necessary for English language learners to participate in classroom activities and function as members of content-centered learning communities. As students develop social and intercultural competence in using English in the classroom, they must also acquire the academic language associated with the content areas of language arts, mathematics, science, and social studies. Thus, both kinds of language proficiency are necessary for school success.

Social, Intercultural, and Instructional Language

In order for English language learners to participate successfully and appropriately in classroom activities, they must learn how to meet classroom expectations. For example, they need to learn how to take turns in instructional conversations with teachers and peers or engage in classroom learning routines. As students develop language proficiency in this area, they have greater access to learning through social interaction and contextualized communication.

In the diverse classrooms of schools throughout the United States, English language learners must also learn how to interact appropriately and effectively with other students and adults from a range of linguistic and cultural backgrounds. They need to develop communication skills that enable them to interact with others in appropriate ways across multiple settings and for a variety of purposes.

> Standard 1 of the English language proficiency standards focuses on these aspects of English language competence.

Academic Language

Academic language refers to the language used to acquire a new or deeper understanding of content related to the core curriculum areas and communicate that understanding to others; it is the language students must use to effectively participate in the classroom environment. Students must be prepared to deal with a range of language demands, such as understanding teachers' oral language and processing textbooks, other print materials, and technological resources. They must also produce language appropriately through oral and written modes for both instruction and assessment. The English language proficiency standards act as a starting point for identifying the language English language learners must develop to successfully access and negotiate content in and beyond the classroom.

Academic language spans several linguistic levels:

- The *word level* (*vocabulary*) consists of words, phrases, and expressions, including general vocabulary students need in classroom routines; nonspecialized, general academic vocabulary encountered in content classes (e.g., *approach, assume,* and *define*); and content-specialized academic vocabulary (e.g., *centimeter* in mathematics and *personification* in language arts).

- The *sentence level (grammar)* consists of language patterns and grammatical structures specific to individual content areas. These may be highly complex and may be encountered primarily in textbooks (e.g., *The attitude revealed in these utterances was apparently not the prevailing one.*).

- The *extended text level (discourse)* includes both general academic structures and discipline-specific genres, such as compare-and-contrast essays, summaries, lab reports for science, and word problems for mathematics.

In keeping with the general principles of language acquisition and current research in classroom language, academic language is addressed in the English language proficiency standards through *academic language functions,* the language required to perform classroom tasks. These functions, such as following directions, writing definitions, and expressing opinions, illustrate how English language learners use language in specific subject areas within grade-level clusters. As students move along the developmental continuum of language proficiency, language demands become greater, linguistic complexity increases, and students must develop facility with a range of informal and formal registers.

> Standards 2, 3, 4, and 5 focus on this aspect of English language competence.

This conceptual framework supports the following major points about the importance of English language proficiency standards in guiding the design of instruction and assessment for English language learners.

1. Language proficiency is an outgrowth of cumulative experiences both inside and outside of school.

2. Language proficiency can reflect complex thinking when linguistic complexity is reduced and support is present.

3. Both social and academic language proficiencies are necessary for school success.

4. Academic language proficiency works in tandem with academic achievement.

5. Academic language proficiency is developed through sustained content-based language instruction.

Considerations in Developing the Standards

Considerations in Developing the Standards

The English language proficiency standards emerged in response to the needs of the growing population of diverse learners for whom English is an additional language throughout the United States.

The English Language Learner Population

Increased Numbers

The rising numbers of English language learners in the United States have created some dramatic changes in schools. For the 1993–1994 school year, the National Clearinghouse for English Language Acquisition (NCELA, http://www.ncela.gwu.edu/) reported the total student enrollment of English language learners as 3,552,497. Ten years later, the total had risen to 4,999,481 school-aged English language learners, a 40.7% increase over the previous decade. States with historically large percentages of English language learners (Arizona, California, Florida, Illinois, New York, Texas) continue to show increases. However, current data also show large and unexpected growth in the number of school-aged English language learners in states that have reported low numbers in the past (e.g., Georgia, Indiana, Nebraska, North Carolina, South Carolina, Tennessee). Although the number of English language learners has been continuously climbing, the number of native-English-speaking, school-aged students in the United States has decreased, making the percentage increase in English language learners even more dramatic.

Diversity

The English language learner population is a microcosm of the total student enrollment across the United States. These learners are a heterogeneous group of students with a variety of learning styles, personalities, and abilities. In addition to being diverse in their languages and cultures, English language learners may come from low- to high-income families or from families with low to high levels of education. English language learners may be gifted in any variety of areas (e.g., academically, musically, artistically), or they may be identified as special needs students with significant disabilities that may require a variety of supplemental services. The length of time it takes English language learners to achieve linguistic and academic parity with native-English-speaking peers may be affected by any of these factors.

The Role of Prior Schooling Experiences (TESOL, 1997)

Students with limited formal schooling are generally recent arrivals to the United States whose backgrounds differ significantly from the school environment they are entering. This category includes students whose schooling has been interrupted for a variety of reasons, including war, poverty, or patterns of migration, as well as students coming from remote rural settings who have had little prior opportunity for sequential schooling. These students may exhibit some of the following characteristics:

- preliteracy or semiliteracy in their native language

- minimal understanding of the functions of literacy

- performance significantly below grade level

- lack of awareness of the organization and culture of school

Many students with limited formal schooling have had little or no exposure to the English language prior to arriving in the United States. It is understandable that these English language learners most likely will not acquire English, especially literacy, at the same pace as students who have had continuous, uninterrupted schooling. Nor do they have the conceptual and experiential backgrounds of peers who have benefited from stable schooling. Although not fully skilled academically, these students possess valuable life skills and experiences that can serve as a basis for academic learning.

Using the English language proficiency standards, the starting place for instruction and assessment for these students is at their designated grade-level cluster. Topics from lower grade-level clusters may be transformed into developmentally appropriate strands, as explained in the section Ways to Implement the Standards. As the English language proficiency standards have been divided into language domains, there are multiple entry points for these students at the beginning levels of English language proficiency.

Anchors for the English Language Proficiency Standards

The English language proficiency standards are grounded in ESL and academic content standards. Figure 4 depicts how both sets of standards have informed the English language

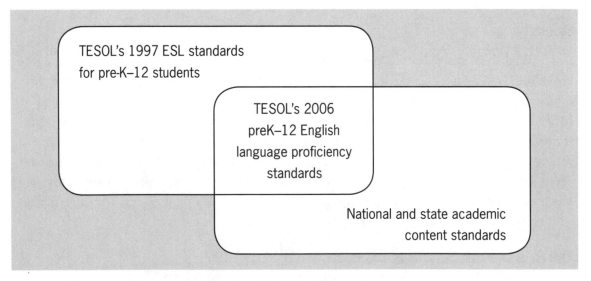

Figure 4. Blending of Standards in the Development of TESOL's
PreK–12 English Language Proficiency Standards

proficiency standards, and Figure 5 shows an index of the national organizations whose content standards were used in developing them.

The English language proficiency standards draw on national and state academic content documents (see Source Documents and References for Further Reading for a list of source documents). Because national standards define the range of competence within each content area, they were used to create frameworks for analyzing a sample of state academic content standards. Furthermore, the English language proficiency standards retain some sample descriptors and progress indicators from TESOL's (1997) ESL standards (see Appendix B for a description of the analysis, alignment, and augmentation process). Evidence of their presence can be found in the strands of sample performance indicators (see Appendix C).

Focus of TESOL's English Language Proficiency Standards	Source of Academic Content Standards
1. Communication in English for social, intercultural, and instructional purposes	Teachers of English to Speakers of Other Languages, Inc.
2. Communication of information, ideas, and concepts of language arts	National Council of Teachers of English and International Reading Association
3. Communication of information, ideas, and concepts of mathematics	National Council of Teachers of Mathematics
4. Communication of information, ideas, and concepts of science	National Research Council
5. Communication of information, ideas, and concepts of social studies	National Council for the Social Studies

Figure 5. Anchors for TESOL's PreK–12 English Language Proficiency Standards

Organization of the Standards

PreK–12
English Language
Proficiency Standards

Standard 1: English language learners **communicate** for **social, intercultural,** and **instructional** purposes within the school setting

Standard 2: English language learners **communicate** information, ideas, and concepts necessary for academic success in the area of **language arts**

Standard 3: English language learners **communicate** information, ideas, and concepts necessary for academic success in the area of **mathematics**

Standard 4: English language learners **communicate** information, ideas, and concepts necessary for academic success in the area of **science**

Standard 5: English language learners **communicate** information, ideas, and concepts necessary for academic success in the area of **social studies**

Organization of the Standards

The five language proficiency standards include both social and academic uses of the language that students must acquire for success in and beyond the classroom. The first standard encompasses social and intercultural interaction along with the language associated with classroom instruction. The other standards target the unique contextual usage of language in the core content areas: language arts, mathematics, science, and social studies. Although not formally recognized within this volume, other content, such as fine arts and physical education, should be considered as part of the overall linguistic, as well as academic, development of English language learners. It is hoped that educators across every content area will draw on the models presented here when working with English language learners.

The English language proficiency standards appear on the opposite page.

The Standards Matrix

The standards and their components are presented in the form of a matrix (see Figure 6). At the top of each matrix is the English language proficiency standard; on the page tab is the designated grade-level cluster, PreK–K, 1–3, 4–5, 6–8, or 9–12.

The matrix consists of a horizontal continuum of five language proficiency levels—Level 1 (Starting), Level 2 (Emerging), Level 3 (Developing), Level 4 (Expanding), and Level 5 (Bridging)—and four language domains—listening, speaking, reading, and writing—displayed vertically. This configuration shows the developmental spectrum of targeted language performance within a specific topic. The selected content topics are representative of national and state academic content standards (see Appendix D for a full list of topics). Native languages and cultures frame the matrix, emphasizing the rich resources English language learners bring to the learning process.

The Standards Matrix

On the page tab is the designated **grade-level cluster**, PreK–K, 1–3, 4–5, 6–8, or 9–12

At the top of each matrix is the **English language proficiency standard**

Grade Level PreK–K

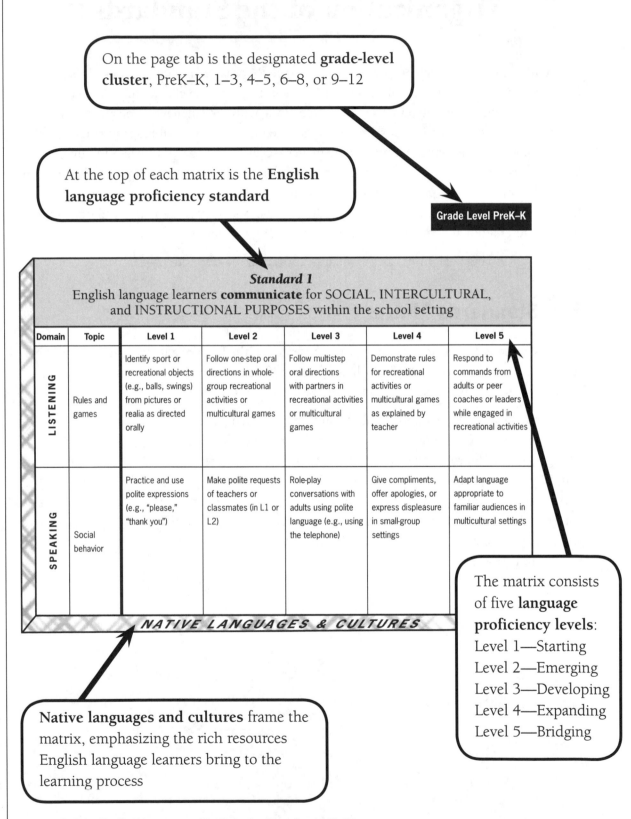

Standard 1
English language learners **communicate** for SOCIAL, INTERCULTURAL, and INSTRUCTIONAL PURPOSES within the school setting

Domain	Topic	Level 1	Level 2	Level 3	Level 4	Level 5
LISTENING	Rules and games	Identify sport or recreational objects (e.g., balls, swings) from pictures or realia as directed orally	Follow one-step oral directions in whole-group recreational activities or multicultural games	Follow multistep oral directions with partners in recreational activities or multicultural games	Demonstrate rules for recreational activities or multicultural games as explained by teacher	Respond to commands from adults or peer coaches or leaders while engaged in recreational activities
SPEAKING	Social behavior	Practice and use polite expressions (e.g., "please," "thank you")	Make polite requests of teachers or classmates (in L1 or L2)	Role-play conversations with adults using polite language (e.g., using the telephone)	Give compliments, offer apologies, or express displeasure in small-group settings	Adapt language appropriate to familiar audiences in multicultural settings

NATIVE LANGUAGES & CULTURES

The matrix consists of five **language proficiency levels**:
Level 1—Starting
Level 2—Emerging
Level 3—Developing
Level 4—Expanding
Level 5—Bridging

Native languages and cultures frame the matrix, emphasizing the rich resources English language learners bring to the learning process

Figure 6. The English Language Proficiency Standards Matrix

		Standard 1 English language learners **communicate** for SOCIAL, INTERCULTURAL, and INSTRUCTIONAL PURPOSES within the school setting				
Domain	**Topic**	**Level 1**	**Level 2**	**Level 3**	**Level 4**	**Level 5**
LISTENING	Rules and games	Identify sport or recreational objects (e.g., balls, swings) from pictures or realia as directed orally	Follow one-step oral directions in whole-group recreational activities or multicultural games	Follow multistep oral directions with partners in recreational activities or multicultural games	Demonstrate rules for recreational activities or multicultural games as explained by teacher	Respond to commands from adults or peer coaches or leaders while engaged in recreational activities
SPEAKING	Social behavior	Practice and use polite expressions (e.g., "please," "thank you")	Make polite requests of teachers or classmates (in L1 or L2)	Role-play conversations with adults using polite language (e.g., using the telephone)	Give compliments, offer apologies, or express displeasure in small-group settings	Adapt language appropriate to familiar audiences in multicultural settings

NATIVE LANGUAGES & CULTURES

The Components of the Standards

Grade-Level Clusters

The grade-level clusters for the English language proficiency standards reflect the current educational configuration or general organization of schools in the United States. Below are the five grade-level clusters with a rationale for their creation.

- *PreK–K:* Educators face increasing accountability for learning during the early school years. By describing the language needed by young students in school, this volume better equips teachers to create learning environments that nurture the language development of young English language learners. In this grade-level cluster, first and second languages may coexist as instructional languages.

- *1–3:* English language learners in primary grades are becoming acclimated to the demands of schooling and developing a strong foundation in literacy, whether in the native language or English. These grade levels are grouped together because in most elementary school programs, this instruction is geared toward learning to read.

- *4–5:* In the middle elementary school years, instruction has shifted to teaching content through literacy. To emphasize this important change in direction, this cluster shares the common goal of literacy skills application, often referred to as reading to learn.

- *6–8:* As most schools in the United States use a middle school organizational structure, this configuration remains as a grade-level cluster. The cluster is characterized by increased academic and social pressures on English language learners as well as a widening range of student performance.

- *9–12:* This grade-level cluster reflects the traditional high school organization. Educators need to acknowledge that the academic demands at the secondary level make reaching parity with grade-level peers increasingly difficult for English language learners. Furthermore, this cluster may represent the widest range of educational experiences.

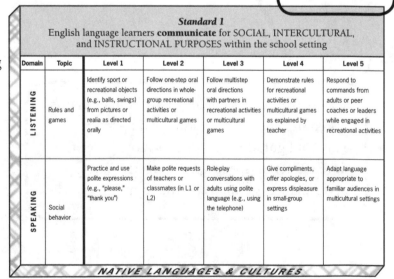

Grade Level PreK–K

Standard 1
English language learners **communicate** for SOCIAL, INTERCULTURAL, and INSTRUCTIONAL PURPOSES within the school setting

Domain	Topic	Level 1	Level 2	Level 3	Level 4	Level 5
LISTENING	Rules and games	Identify sport or recreational objects (e.g., balls, swings) from pictures or realia as directed orally	Follow one-step oral directions in whole-group recreational activities or multicultural games	Follow multistep oral directions with partners in recreational activities or multicultural games	Demonstrate rules for recreational activities or multicultural games as explained by teacher	Respond to commands from adults or peer coaches or leaders while engaged in recreational activities
SPEAKING	Social behavior	Practice and use polite expressions (e.g., "please," "thank you")	Make polite requests of teachers or classmates (in L1 or L2)	Role-play conversations with adults using polite language (e.g., using the telephone)	Give compliments, offer apologies, or express displeasure in small-group settings	Adapt language appropriate to familiar audiences in multicultural settings

NATIVE LANGUAGES & CULTURES

Language Domains

Each language proficiency standard is divided into the language domains of listening, speaking, reading, and writing. Although interaction naturally occurs between and among language domains, in this volume they are maintained as separate constructs as one way of thinking about curriculum, instruction, and assessment.

Listening

English language learners process, understand, and respond to spoken language from a variety of speakers for a range of purposes in a variety of situations. Listening is not a passive skill; input for listening includes students' viewing of materials as well as their internalizing of oral information from teachers, other adults, and peers. Highlighting an assortment of listening tasks across standards makes clear the need to involve students in developing active listening and purposeful listening skills.

Speaking

English language learners engage in oral communication in a variety of situations for a variety of purposes and audiences in a wide spectrum of social, cultural, and academic contexts. As part of oral communication, students are constantly using language in purposeful and meaningful interaction with others.

Reading

English language learners process, interpret, and evaluate written language, symbols, and text with understanding and fluency. Students' level of literacy in their native languages may enhance or hinder the process of learning to read in a second language. Students who have a strong foundation in reading in their first language bring with them skills that can be readily transferred to learning to read in English.

Writing

English language learners engage in written communication in a variety of forms for a variety of purposes and audiences. These forms include expressing meaning through drawing, symbols, or text. English language learners may come to school with writing styles influenced by their home cultures.

Standard 1
English language learners **communicate** for SOCIAL, INTERCULTURAL, and INSTRUCTIONAL PURPOSES within the school setting

Domain	Topic	Level 1	Level 2	Level 3	Level 4	Level 5
LISTENING	Rules and games	Identify sport or recreational objects (e.g., balls, swings) from pictures or realia as directed orally	Follow one-step oral directions in whole-group recreational activities or multicultural games	Follow multistep oral directions with partners in recreational activities or multicultural games	Demonstrate rules for recreational activities or multicultural games as explained by teacher	Respond to commands from adults or peer coaches or leaders while engaged in recreational activities
SPEAKING	Social behavior	Practice and use polite expressions (e.g., "please," "thank you")	Make polite requests of teachers or classmates (in L1 or L2)	Role-play conversations with adults using polite language (e.g., using the telephone)	Give compliments, offer apologies, or express displeasure in small-group settings	Adapt language appropriate to familiar audiences in multicultural settings

NATIVE LANGUAGES & CULTURES

Native Languages and Cultures

Students' proficiency in their native languages contributes to the successful development of additional languages. While acquiring English, most students remain immersed in their native language and home culture, thereby enriching the learning process. The frame surrounding the matrices represents how native languages and cultures frame English language learners' experiences in language development. This resource is to be tapped and integrated into instruction and assessment. As stated in TESOL's Vision of Effective Education for All Students (see the Conceptual Framework section), knowledge of more than one language and culture is a societal asset, and learning English as an additional language should neither replace nor diminish the value of students' native languages and cultures.

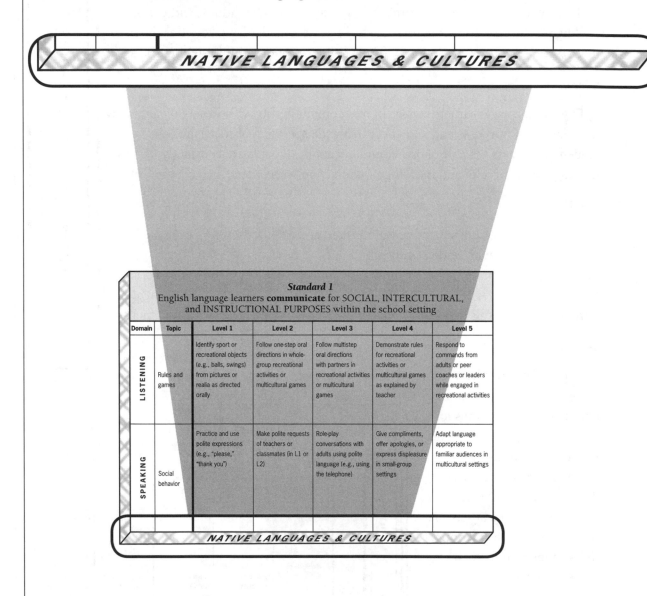

NATIVE LANGUAGES & CULTURES

Standard 1
English language learners **communicate** for SOCIAL, INTERCULTURAL, and INSTRUCTIONAL PURPOSES within the school setting

Domain	Topic	Level 1	Level 2	Level 3	Level 4	Level 5
LISTENING	Rules and games	Identify sport or recreational objects (e.g., balls, swings) from pictures or realia as directed orally	Follow one-step oral directions in whole-group recreational activities or multicultural games	Follow multistep oral directions with partners in recreational activities or multicultural games	Demonstrate rules for recreational activities or multicultural games as explained by teacher	Respond to commands from adults or peer coaches or leaders while engaged in recreational activities
SPEAKING	Social behavior	Practice and use polite expressions (e.g., "please," "thank you")	Make polite requests of teachers or classmates (in L1 or L2)	Role-play conversations with adults using polite language (e.g., using the telephone)	Give compliments, offer apologies, or express displeasure in small-group settings	Adapt language appropriate to familiar audiences in multicultural settings

NATIVE LANGUAGES & CULTURES

Content Topics

Content topics are drawn from an analysis of national and state academic content standards in ESL, language arts, mathematics, science, and social studies (see Source Documents and References for Further Reading; see Appendix D for a complete list of topics). These topics are a window into the language demands of these content areas. They provide a starting point for determining the language objectives that need to accompany content objectives for instruction and assessment.

Many content topics spiral and repeat over grade-level clusters; however, for the most part, they are listed when first introduced in national and state academic content standards. The curriculum broadens with each successive cluster. In general, preK–K curricula are organized around themes rather than distinct topics. In subsequent grade-level clusters, multiple topics offer a choice of content across the language proficiency levels. In addition, the language arts standards suggest types of genres most typically addressed within a grade-level cluster.

A topic or a series of topics introduces a strand of sample performance indicators within a language domain. In the graphic below, we see a single topic for listening (Rules and games) and speaking (Social behavior). Often, however, there are multiple topics that may apply to a strand within a language domain; each topic is independent and begins with a capital letter. For example, on page 73, suggested topics for English language proficiency standard 3 (the language of mathematics), for reading, include Three-dimensional shapes, Polygons, and Angles.

ain	Topic	
	Rules and games	Ide rec (e. fro rea or
	Social behavior	Pr po (e. "th

Standard 1
English language learners **communicate** for SOCIAL, INTERCULTURAL, and INSTRUCTIONAL PURPOSES within the school setting

Domain	Topic	Level 1	Level 2	Level 3	Level 4	Level 5
LISTENING	Rules and games	Identify sport or recreational objects (e.g., balls, swings) from pictures or realia as directed orally	Follow one-step oral directions in whole-group recreational activities or multicultural games	Follow multistep oral directions with partners in recreational activities or multicultural games	Demonstrate rules for recreational activities or multicultural games as explained by teacher	Respond to commands from adults or peer coaches or leaders while engaged in recreational activities
SPEAKING	Social behavior	Practice and use polite expressions (e.g., "please," "thank you")	Make polite requests of teachers or classmates (in L1 or L2)	Role-play conversations with adults using polite language (e.g., using the telephone)	Give compliments, offer apologies, or express displeasure in small-group settings	Adapt language appropriate to familiar audiences in multicultural settings

NATIVE LANGUAGES & CULTURES

Levels of Language Proficiency

In the English language proficiency standards, the range of language proficiency is represented by five levels. The use of five levels reflects the complexity of language development and allows the documenting of student progress across grade levels within the same scale over time. Language proficiency scales typically use multiple levels. The American Council of Teachers of Foreign Languages' (ACTFL, 1986) scales, for example, cover five levels, whereas the Council of Europe's (2001) *Common European Framework* includes six levels.

ic	Level 1	Level 2	Level 3	Level 4	Level 5
	Identify sport or	Follow one-step oral	Follow multistep	Demonstrate rules	Respond to

Standard 1
English language learners **communicate** for SOCIAL, INTERCULTURAL, and INSTRUCTIONAL PURPOSES within the school setting

Domain	Topic	Level 1	Level 2	Level 3	Level 4	Level 5
LISTENING	Rules and games	Identify sport or recreational objects (e.g., balls, swings) from pictures or realia as directed orally	Follow one-step oral directions in whole-group recreational activities or multicultural games	Follow multistep oral directions with partners in recreational activities or multicultural games	Demonstrate rules for recreational activities or multicultural games as explained by teacher	Respond to commands from adults or peer coaches or leaders while engaged in recreational activities
SPEAKING	Social behavior	Practice and use polite expressions (e.g., "please," "thank you")	Make polite requests of teachers or classmates (in L1 or L2)	Role-play conversations with adults using polite language (e.g., using the telephone)	Give compliments, offer apologies, or express displeasure in small-group settings	Adapt language appropriate to familiar audiences in multicultural settings

NATIVE LANGUAGES & CULTURES

Figure 7 depicts the five levels of language proficiency as a series of stepping-stones along a developmental continuum. The five levels used in this volume are not based on a particular length of time but rather reflect characteristics of language performance at each developmental stage. The language proficiency levels are intended to provide a model illustrating that language acquisition is a predictable, developmental process. School districts and states may adapt this model to their own language-leveling system.

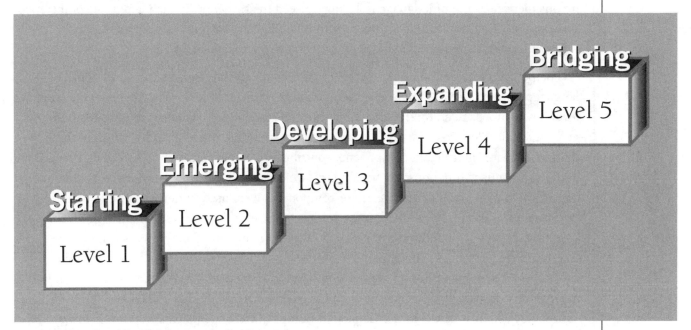

Figure 7. Levels of English Language Proficiency

The English language proficiency standards matrices use a new set of labels—*Starting, Emerging, Developing, Expanding*, and *Bridging*—to characterize language proficiency levels. While TESOL recognizes the variety of existing labels for language proficiency across states and school districts, these labels focus on the developmental nature of language learning and acknowledge the individual nature of each stage rather than viewing one level as a subset of other levels in a continuum (e.g., *beginning, advanced beginning; early intermediate, late intermediate*). Grade-level clusters address multiple grade levels. The descriptors included in the sample performance indicators at Level 5 are representative of the highest grade level (or benchmark) included in any given span; for example, in grade-level cluster 1–3, Grade 3 is the benchmark grade level. Additionally, skills included in the sample performance indicator are not meant to be viewed as exit criteria but rather to reflect what English language learners know and are able to do with language at that proficiency level.

Note that English language learners may perform at different language proficiency levels in different language domains at the same time. Learners may exhibit a high level of oral proficiency, for example, but their literacy skills may be at a lower level, or the converse. Students at Level 5 in speaking may not necessarily be at that level in writing even though both are productive skills. In the same way, students may develop language proficiency at varying rates, thus moving through each continuum at different paces.

The language proficiency levels are not an index of cognitive functioning. Cognitive involvement required of language tasks may exceed the students' English language competence. For example, English language learners with little English can still analyze and classify information if it is presented in small chunks and supported visually.

The performance definitions in Figure 8 describe the overall expectations for English language learners' use of language at each language proficiency level. They connect the language level descriptions, given on the following pages, to student performances in the classroom and are applicable across the domains of listening, speaking, reading, and writing. In these definitions, four interrelated components contribute to communication in English: (1) social and academic language functions; (2) vocabulary (words, phrases, and expressions); (3) grammar; and (4) discourse (extended text). These components were used in developing the sample performance indicators described in the section Matrices of Sample Performance Indicators. They also provide a direction for the design of lesson plans and classroom assessments for English language learners. Examples of how these components can act as a springboard for instructional assessment design are given in Ways to Implement the Standards. The definitions are informed in part by descriptions of language proficiency found in the Global Scale of the Common Reference Levels in the Council of Europe's (2001) *Common European Framework*.

Level 1 Starting	Level 2 Emerging	Level 3 Developing	Level 4 Expanding	Level 5 Bridging
English language learners can understand and use ...				
... language to communicate with others around basic concrete needs.	... language to draw on simple and routine experiences to communicate with others.	... language to communicate with others on familiar matters regularly encountered.	... language in both concrete and abstract situations and apply language to new experiences.	... a wide range of longer oral and written texts and recognize implicit meaning.
... high-frequency words and memorized chunks of language.	... high-frequency and some general academic vocabulary and expressions.	... general and some specialized academic vocabulary and expressions.	... specialized and some technical academic vocabulary and expressions.	... technical academic vocabulary and expressions.
... words, phrases, or chunks of language.	... phrases or short sentences in oral or written communication.	... expanded sentences in oral or written communication.	... a variety of sentence lengths of varying linguistic complexity in oral and written communication.	... a variety of sentence lengths of varying linguistic complexity in extended oral or written discourse.
... pictorial, graphic, or nonverbal representation of language.	... oral or written language, making errors that often impede the meaning of the communication.	... oral or written language, making errors that may impede the communication but retain much of its meaning.	... oral or written language, making minimal errors that do not impede the overall meaning of the communication.	... oral or written language approaching comparability to that of English-proficient peers.

Figure 8. Performance Definitions of the Five Levels of English Language Proficiency

Level 1: Starting

At the Starting level, students initially have little to no understanding of English and rarely use English for communication. They respond nonverbally to simple commands, statements, and questions. As their oral comprehension increases, they begin to imitate the verbalizations of others by using single words or simple phrases, and begin to use English spontaneously. At the earliest stage, learners construct meaning from text primarily through nonprint features (e.g., illustrations, graphs, maps, tables). They gradually construct more meaning from the words themselves, but the construction is often incomplete. They are able to generate simple texts that reflect their knowledge level of syntax. These texts may include a significant amount of nonconventional features, such as invented spelling, grammatical inaccuracies, pictorial representations, and surface features and rhetorical patterns of the native language (such as replication of ways of structuring text from the native culture and language).

Level 2: Emerging

At the Emerging level, students can understand phrases and short sentences. They can communicate limited information in simple, everyday and routine situations by using memorized phrases, groups of words, and formulae. They can use selected simple structures correctly, but still systematically produce basic errors. Students at this level begin to use general academic vocabulary and familiar, everyday expressions.

Reading and writing proficiency may vary depending on students' literacy development in their native language and their familiarity with the alphabet, among other factors. Students can read words and phrases and locate specific, predictable information in simple everyday or environmental print. They often make errors in writing that hinder communication.

Level 3: Developing

At the Developing level, students understand more complex speech but may still require some repetition. They acquire a vocabulary of stock words and phrases covering many daily situations. They use English spontaneously but may have difficulty expressing all their thoughts because of a restricted vocabulary and a limited command of language structure. Students at this level speak in simple sentences that are comprehensible and appropriate but that are frequently marked by grammatical errors. Although they may understand and use some specialized academic vocabulary, they still have some trouble comprehending and producing complex structures and academic language.

Proficiency in reading may vary considerably depending upon the learners' familiarity and prior experiences with themes, concepts, or genres. They are most successful constructing meaning from texts for which they have background knowledge on which to build. In writing, they are able to generate more complex texts, a wider variety of texts, and more coherent texts than are learners at the Starting and Emerging levels. Texts still have considerable numbers of nonconventional features.

Level 4: Expanding

At the Expanding level, students' language skills are adequate for most day-to-day communication needs. Occasional structural and lexical errors occur. Students may have difficulty understanding and using some idioms, figures of speech, and words with multiple meanings. They communicate in English in new or unfamiliar settings but have occasional difficulty with complex structures and abstract academic concepts.

Students at this level may read with considerable fluency and are able to locate and identify specific facts within the text. However, they may not understand texts in which the concepts are presented in a decontextualized manner, the sentence structure is complex, or the vocabulary is abstract or has multiple meanings. They can read independently but may have occasional comprehension problems, especially when processing grade-level information. Although students can produce texts independently for personal and academic purposes, they encounter more difficulty with grade-level literacy than with oral language. Structures, vocabulary, and overall organization begin to approximate the writing of native speakers of English. Errors, however, may persist in one or more language domains, but they generally do not interfere with communication.

Level 5: Bridging

Students at the Bridging level are not necessarily fully English proficient, especially across all language domains and all standards. Students can express themselves fluently and spontaneously on a wide range of personal, general, academic, or social topics in a variety of contexts. They are poised to function effectively in an environment with native-English-speaking peers with minimal language support or guidance.

At this level, students are able to work with grade-level material with some modification. They have a good command of technical and academic vocabulary as well as idiomatic expressions and colloquialisms. Students can produce clear, smoothly flowing, well-structured texts of differing lengths and degrees of linguistic complexity. Errors are minimal, may be difficult to spot, and are generally corrected when they occur.

Sample Performance Indicators

As their name implies, sample performance indicators are examples of observable, measurable language behaviors that English language learners can be expected to demonstrate as they engage in classroom tasks and approach the transition to the next level of English language proficiency. The sample performance indicators are found in the cells within the matrices illustrating each standard and are formed by the interaction of the levels of language proficiency and language domains. As students engage in classroom tasks, teachers can observe English language learners' progress in moving toward language and content objectives through the language behaviors exhibited in the sample performance indicators. Representative of a range of possible language behaviors, sample performance indicators are intended to be descriptive, not prescriptive, and dynamic, not static.

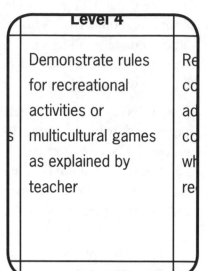

Level 4

Demonstrate rules for recreational activities or multicultural games as explained by teacher

		Standard 1				
		English language learners **communicate** for SOCIAL, INTERCULTURAL, and INSTRUCTIONAL PURPOSES within the school setting				
Domain	Topic	Level 1	Level 2	Level 3	Level 4	Level 5
LISTENING	Rules and games	Identify sport or recreational objects (e.g., balls, swings) from pictures or realia as directed orally	Follow one-step oral directions in whole-group recreational activities or multicultural games	Follow multistep oral directions with partners in recreational activities or multicultural games	Demonstrate rules for recreational activities or multicultural games as explained by teacher	Respond to commands from adults or peer coaches or leaders while engaged in recreational activities
SPEAKING	Social behavior	Practice and use polite expressions (e.g., "please," "thank you")	Make polite requests of teachers or classmates (in L1 or L2)	Role-play conversations with adults using polite language (e.g., using the telephone)	Give compliments, offer apologies, or express displeasure in small-group settings	Adapt language appropriate to familiar audiences in multicultural settings

NATIVE LANGUAGES & CULTURES

Sample performance indicators generally consist of three elements (see Figure 9). The first, the *content* of communication, denotes content information. The topics for sample performance indicators have been drawn from thorough analyses of national and state academic content standards. Examples of topics include *measures of central tendency* for Standard 3—the language of mathematics—and *interests and opinions* for Standard 1—social, intercultural, and instructional language. The second element, *language function*, states how students use language in communicating a message within the designated standard. Examples of language functions are *justify and defend* and *interpret*. The last element specifies some type of *support or strategy* associated with the communication act. Examples of supports or strategies are visual, graphic, or interactional, as in *using manipulatives, completing organizers*, or *working in small groups*. Classroom applications or subtopics of sample performance indicators are in parentheses (see Figure 6).

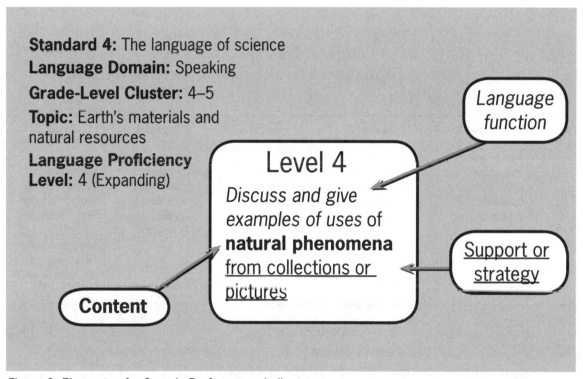

Standard 4: The language of science
Language Domain: Speaking
Grade-Level Cluster: 4–5
Topic: Earth's materials and natural resources
Language Proficiency Level: 4 (Expanding)

Level 4

Discuss and give examples of uses of **natural phenomena** from collections or pictures

Language function

Support or strategy

Content

Figure 9. Elements of a Sample Performance Indicator

A variety of supports or strategies are presented in the matrices, appearing at Levels 1–4. Support is continued with Level 5 for younger learners; for older students, support is often provided through modified grade-level material. With instruction that supports students visually, graphically, or interactively and gives them multiple avenues to access meaning, English language learners are able to engage in higher levels of cognitive involvement within lower levels of English language proficiency. However, it cannot be assumed that students automatically know how to use these strategies. The use of strategies must be explicitly taught to ensure that students benefit from the support.

Strands of Sample Performance Indicators

The sample performance indicators form a strand in a developmental chain across the five language proficiency levels.

In the first example in Figure 10, for grade-level cluster 1–3, the linguistic complexity increases (from words, to phrases, to sentences, to extended text or discourse) from one language proficiency level to the next. The second example in Figure 10 shows a strand of sample performance indicators designed for older students. In this series of language proficiency levels, the language functions (*exchange, share, discuss, explain, give*) help shape the kinds of language patterns used within the specified context or topic, in this case, information about human populations.

The matrices in the following section show the strands by language domain for each grade-level cluster and English language proficiency standard.

Standard 3
English language learners communicate information, ideas, and concepts necessary for academic success in the area of MATHEMATICS

Domain	Topic	Level 1	Level 2	Level 3	Level 4	Level 5	
READING	Basic operations	Identify **words** associated with symbols for addition, subtraction, or multiplication with a partner (e.g., + goes with "and" or "plus")	Locate or sort **phrases** associated with symbols for addition, subtraction, or multiplication with a partner (e.g., "Twelve *take away* two is ten.")	Select and categorize by operation equivalent **phrases or sentences** in illustrated text with a partner	Arrange **sentences** in logical order to create illustrated story problems with a partner	Analyze **extended text** to find clues for problem solving (e.g., "There are six red balls *and* two green balls. How many balls are there *in all?*")	Grade Level 1–3

Standard 5
English language learners communicate information, ideas, and concepts necessary for academic success in the area of SOCIAL STUDIES

Domain	Topic	Level 1	Level 2	Level 3	Level 4	Level 5	
SPEAKING	Human populations	**Exchange** facts about the peoples, languages, or cultures of local communities or native countries with a partner (using L1 or L2)	**Share** personal experiences and reactions to migration/immigration with a partner	**Discuss** demographic shifts, migration/immigration patterns, languages or cultures in small groups	**Explain** the impact of demographic shifts or migration/immigration patterns on peoples, languages, or cultures in small groups	**Give** multimedia demonstrations, speeches, or presentations on characteristics, distribution, and migration of peoples, their languages, and their cultures	Grade Level 9–12

Figure 10. Examples of Strands of Sample Performance Indicators

Matrices
of Sample
Performance
Indicators

Matrices of Sample Performance Indicators

The matrices are organized by standard and grade-level cluster. They are formed by the interaction of the five language proficiency levels with each language domain. Oral language (listening and speaking) strands of sample performance indicators for each standard and grade level are on one page followed by those for literacy development (reading and writing) on the next. The topics introduce possible content-based themes that have been derived from national and state academic content standards.

The matrices elucidate how the English language proficiency standards may be utilized in preK–12 classrooms with English language learners of varying levels of English language proficiency. Figure 11 points out the features of the matrices and clarifies their uses. Although each example within a cell of the matrices is unique for the grade-level cluster and language domain, it may readily be modified to best serve the needs of the students and their teachers (see Ways to Implement the Standards for suggestions).

The Sample Performance Indicators. . .

. . . ARE examples of how to operationalize the English language proficiency standards.	. . . ARE NOT the standards themselves.
. . . ARE expected performance at the end of a given level of language proficiency.	. . . ARE NOT activities or tasks per se.
. . . ARE ideas for scaffolding or differentiating language instruction.	. . . ARE NOT a de facto curriculum.
. . . ARE flexible and dynamic elements, intended to be combined across standards or language domains, or interchanged or substituted according to contexts of instruction.	. . . ARE NOT fixed or unalterable language functions, topics, supports, or strategies.

Figure 11. What Are the Sample Performance Indicators?

Standard 1

English language learners **communicate** for SOCIAL, INTERCULTURAL, and INSTRUCTIONAL PURPOSES within the school setting

Domain	Topic	Level 1	Level 2	Level 3	Level 4	Level 5
LISTENING	Rules and games	Identify sport or recreational objects (e.g., balls, swings) from pictures or realia as directed orally	Follow one-step oral directions in whole-group recreational activities or multicultural games	Follow multistep oral directions with partners in recreational activities or multicultural games	Demonstrate rules for recreational activities or multicultural games as explained by teacher	Respond to commands from adults or peer coaches or leaders while engaged in recreational activities
SPEAKING	Social behavior	Practice and use polite expressions (e.g., "please," "thank you")	Make polite requests of teachers or classmates (in L1 or L2)	Role-play conversations with adults using polite language (e.g., using the telephone)	Give compliments, offer apologies, or express displeasure in small-group settings	Adapt language appropriate to familiar audiences in multicultural settings

NATIVE LANGUAGES & CULTURES

Standard 1

English language learners **communicate** for SOCIAL, INTERCULTURAL, and INSTRUCTIONAL PURPOSES within the school setting

Domain	Topic	Level 1	Level 2	Level 3	Level 4	Level 5
READING	Classroom	Match words with pictures on word walls, bulletin boards (in L1 or L2) to words in print	Identify letters in the names of classroom objects illustrated and in print	Match names of familiar objects with pictures or realia	Identify words or phrases in the school environment (e.g., "Exit," "Office")	Construct meaning from illustrated books with text
WRITING	Family	Depict family members in drawings	Label drawings or photos of family members or friends using letters or scribble writings	Describe family members using a combination of drawings, letters, scribble writings, or words with inverted spellings	Represent stories of family experiences using a combination of drawings, letters, words, and phrases with invented spellings	Copy and illustrate notes to family members using a combination of words and phrases with invented spellings

NATIVE LANGUAGES & CULTURES

Standard 2

English language learners **communicate** information, ideas, and concepts necessary for academic success in the area of LANGUAGE ARTS

Domain	Topic	Level 1	Level 2	Level 3	Level 4	Level 5
LISTENING	Colors	Respond nonverbally to oral directions (e.g., "Get the red ball.") as part of whole-group activities	Identify realia or objects in pictures in books from oral descriptions by teachers or adults (e.g., pointing to "Brown bear, brown bear")	Place realia in locations according to descriptive oral directions (e.g., "Put the bright blue paper on my desk.")	Arrange series of pictures or objects according to descriptive oral directions that include compound sentences	Organize pictures according to descriptive oral discourse to create collages or displays
SPEAKING	Community helpers	State occupations (e.g., firefighters, police), in L1 or L2, from pictures or illustrated books	Relate occupations to tools of their trade through pictures of community scenes	Ask and answer wh- questions in small groups about occupations (e.g., "What does a mail carrier do?")	Role-play occupations using props and phrases or short sentences	Describe class field trips or experiences (e.g., to a police station or firehouse) using complete sentences

NATIVE LANGUAGES & CULTURES

Standard 2

English language learners **communicate** information, ideas, and concepts necessary for academic success in the area of LANGUAGE ARTS

Domain	Topic	Level 1	Level 2	Level 3	Level 4	Level 5
READING	Feelings Concepts about print	Match symbols or icons with photographs or facial expressions that express feelings (e.g., a happy face)	Match letters with pictures that express feelings with a partner	Match words with pictures that express feelings with a partner	Sequence a series of picture cards with text to create a story (e.g., "The Sad Prince")	Predict feelings associated with grade-level stories based on titles and illustrations
WRITING	Animals and their habitats	Draw, copy, or trace animals from familiar materials	Represent familiar animal habitats using recognizable drawings, letters, and scribble writings	Reproduce words, along with drawings, from animal rhymes, songs, or classroom books	Tell about animal habitats using a combination of drawings, letters, words, and phrases with invented spellings	Create stories about animals using a combination of drawings, words, and phrases with invented spellings

NATIVE LANGUAGES & CULTURES

Standard 3

English language learners **communicate** information, ideas, and concepts necessary for academic success in the area of MATHEMATICS

Domain	Topic	Level 1	Level 2	Level 3	Level 4	Level 5
LISTENING	Patterns	Imitate pattern sounds with physical movement (e.g., clap, snap, snap, stomp) in a whole group	Identify patterns in the environment based on oral descriptions (in L1 or L2)	Select "What comes next?" in illustrated patterns or sequences according to oral directions	Follow short oral directions to form patterns using manipulatives (e.g., "Put two big tiles next to a small one.") with a partner	Follow detailed oral directions to extend patterns using manipulatives
SPEAKING	Numbers and operations	Use number words to count (up to 10) objects (e.g., candies, crayons) with a partner	Repeat phrases involving addition and subtraction (e.g., in choral chants such as "Five Little Monkeys")	Use comparative phrases (e.g., "more than," "less than," "bigger") with a partner to describe the relationship between two objects	Pose comparative questions (e.g., "What is one more than ...?") to classmates	Discuss grade-level math stories using comparative language (e.g., "one more," "less than," "more than")

NATIVE LANGUAGES & CULTURES

Standard 3

English language learners **communicate** information, ideas, and concepts necessary for academic success in the area of MATHEMATICS

Domain	Topic	Level 1	Level 2	Level 3	Level 4	Level 5
READING	Measurement Geometry	Match pictures or icons with realia (e.g., wheels or sails) in small groups	Order pictures or realia with a partner according to observable, measurable attributes	Categorize labeled pictures (e.g., circle, square, or rectangle) according to observable, measurable attributes	Find matching shape words from different sources (e.g., on word walls, in big books) with a partner	Identify words for shapes, order, or position from pictures, flash cards, and word walls
WRITING	Time Calendar	Draw pictures from models to express times of day (e.g., day or night)	Create drawings and writings that include letters and scribble writings about morning, noon, and night	Create drawings and writings that include letters, scribble writings, and words with invented spellings to depict special times of day	Contribute to whole-class activities to create stories or books about a time-related sequence of events	Produce illustrated stories about a time-related sequence of events using drawings, words, phrases, and invented spellings

NATIVE LANGUAGES & CULTURES

Standard 4

English language learners **communicate** information, ideas, and concepts necessary for academic success in the area of SCIENCE

Domain	Topic	Level 1	Level 2	Level 3	Level 4	Level 5
LISTENING	Living and nonliving things	Identify living or nonliving things by using pictures or finding realia named by teachers	Follow oral directions to collect and display pictures and realia (e.g., "Put the shells on the table.")	Respond to *wh-* questions or oral descriptions using pictures or realia	Sort and match features (e.g, feathers/birds, fur/dogs, skin/ people) according to pictures and oral directions	Organize pictures of organisms with labels or other graphic representations according to observable features described orally
SPEAKING	Seasons Weather	Name realia or pictures associated with various times of the year (e.g., clothing, food)	Describe seasonal activities in home country or the United States from illustrations (and L1 support)	Answer *wh-* questions about photos or illustrations of different seasons or weather	Contrast characteristics of seasons or weather using photos or illustrations	Discuss likes and dislikes about seasons or weather

NATIVE LANGUAGES & CULTURES

Standard 4

English language learners **communicate** information, ideas, and concepts necessary for academic success in the area of SCIENCE

Domain	Topic	Level 1	Level 2	Level 3	Level 4	Level 5
READING	Senses	Apply concepts about print to identify different senses in picture books	Sort pictures according to labels and icons of the senses	Classify visual representations of activities according to the labels and icons of the senses (e.g., see or watch a movie)	Infer or predict sensory responses to scenes in picture books (e.g., "That place is cold" or "That skunk smells stinky.")	Compare information in picture or grade-level books about the senses
WRITING	Scientific inquiry	Reproduce, trace, or copy pictures based on observations during class activities	Produce drawings and labels with letters and scribble writings based on observations during class activities	Copy or create a list of materials (e.g., for growing seeds) using a combination of drawings, letters, scribble writings, and words with invented spellings	Describe steps for inquiry using a combination of drawings, words, or phrases with invented spellings	Produce stories about class experiences (e.g., planting seeds) using a combination of drawings, words, and phrases with invented spellings

NATIVE LANGUAGES & CULTURES

Standard 5

English language learners **communicate** information, ideas, and concepts necessary for academic success in the area of SOCIAL STUDIES

Domain	Topic	Level 1	Level 2	Level 3	Level 4	Level 5
LISTENING	Transportation (in the neighborhood)	Match sounds of different modes of transportation with their pictures	Gesture or role-play in response to group songs or chants (e.g., "The Wheels on the Bus")	Pantomime or role-play various transportation scenes as directed (e.g., "An airplane goes fast.") in small groups	Create different types of vehicles (e.g., a cardboard bus or a car from blocks) according to teacher directions in teams or groups	Identify types of transportation from the past or present from oral descriptions
SPEAKING	Homes/ habitats	Repeat names of different types of homes or habitats from pictures (e.g., nest, house)	Describe homes or habitats as part of rhymes, chants, and songs in a large group	Recite predictable sentence patterns that have visual support (e.g., "A bird lives in a nest.")	Compare different types of homes or habitats found in nonfiction picture books	Provide information on location and directionality of homes or habitats (e.g., "… up in a tree," "… next to my house")

NATIVE LANGUAGES & CULTURES

Standard 5

English language learners **communicate** information, ideas, and concepts necessary for academic success in the area of SOCIAL STUDIES

Domain	Topic	Level 1	Level 2	Level 3	Level 4	Level 5
READING	School	Identify (in L1 or L2) pictures of various locations in the school as part of a group activity	Match names of various school workers with pictures from multiple sources (e.g., big books)	Sort labeled pictures of classroom objects by initial letters	Identify, with a partner, capital letters from a list of names of school workers	Identify vocabulary words in illustrated phrases and short sentences
WRITING	Self Friends Family	Draw pictures of shared experiences with a friend	Label pictures of self, friends, or family members using a combination of letters and scribble writings	Draw and label familiar people or places using pictures and a combination of scribble writing, letters, and words with invented spellings	Make illustrated lists of familiar people or places in pairs or triads using a combination of letters, words, and phrases with invented spellings	Create picture books or stories with a partner using a combination of words and phrases with invented spellings

NATIVE LANGUAGES & CULTURES

Standard 1

English language learners **communicate** for SOCIAL, INTERCULTURAL, and INSTRUCTIONAL purposes within the school setting

Domain	Topic	Level 1	Level 2	Level 3	Level 4	Level 5
LISTENING	Directions Instructions	Mimic responses to one-step oral commands supported by gestures, songs, or realia	Follow one- to two-step oral commands supported by gestures, songs, or realia	Follow a series of oral commands supported by gestures, songs, or realia	Follow multistep commands within oral discourse supported by gestures or realia	Follow multistep commands within oral discourse in various contexts
SPEAKING	Feelings Emotions Needs	Respond to everyday oral requests or questions from a partner	Make requests, ask questions, or state reactions to everyday events, situations, or cultural experiences with a partner	Describe or recount reactions to everyday events, situations, or cultural experiences in small groups	Elaborate, using details or examples, reactions to events, situations, or cultural experiences	Present skits reflecting reactions to events, situations, or cultural experiences

NATIVE LANGUAGES & CULTURES

Standard 1

English language learners **communicate** for SOCIAL, INTERCULTURAL, and INSTRUCTIONAL purposes within the school setting

Domain	Topic	Level 1	Level 2	Level 3	Level 4	Level 5
READING	Messages Information	Match icons of home, school, or community with individual words with a partner	Associate icons of home, school, or community with phrases or short sentences expressing their functions (e.g., "Cars stop here.") with a partner	Answer or select questions related to icons, illustrated announcements, invitations, or memos (e.g., "When is the fair?") with a partner	Connect facts or ideas in illustrated announcements, invitations, or memos to new situations with a partner	Infer facts or ideas in illustrated announcements, invitations, or memos
WRITING	Social, cultural, school traditions	Label or match names of peers, teachers, or family members in person or photographs	Create illustrated lists by brainstorming special events or celebrations at school, home, or home country with a partner or in small groups	Describe special events or celebrations at school, home, or home country using drawings or graphic organizers	Explain and give details of special events or celebrations at school, home, or in the home country using drawings or graphic organizers	Produce stories about special events or celebrations and share with peers

NATIVE LANGUAGES & CULTURES

Standard 2

English language learners **communicate** information, ideas, and concepts necessary for academic success in the area of LANGUAGE ARTS

Domain	Topic	Level 1	Level 2	Level 3	Level 4	Level 5
LISTENING	Phonics Phonemic awareness	Identify sounds, syllables, or compound words nonverbally (e.g., by clapping) in small groups	Discriminate between regular and irregular words (e.g., count nouns or past tense) through gestures in oral sentences with a partner	Identify affixes, root words, and derivational endings through gestures in oral discourse with a partner	Replicate through gestures, stress, and intonation patterns of rhymes, prose, or poetry with a partner	Identify the musical elements of literary language (e.g., rhymes, repeated sounds, or onomatopoeia) through simulation
SPEAKING	Rhyming words	Practice saying illustrated word pairs with a partner (e.g., "The boy has a toy.")	Repeat phrases or chants with illustrated referents in large or small groups	Create sentences or chants based on familiar word families or topics in small groups	Perform rhymes, raps, or verses developed with a partner	Recite original raps, verses, or poetry

NATIVE LANGUAGES & CULTURES

Standard 2

English language learners **communicate** information, ideas, and concepts necessary for academic success in the area of LANGUAGE ARTS

Domain	Topic	Level 1	Level 2	Level 3	Level 4	Level 5
READING	Story grammar	Identify story elements with visual support by names (characters) or places (settings)	Categorize story elements with visual support using graphic organizers by description of characters, settings, or events	Sequence story events with visually supported text by beginning, middle, and end	Match transition words (e.g., "finally") or phrases with sequence, main ideas, or details in visually supported stories	Identify and order main ideas and details, using modified grade-level stories
WRITING	Homophones Compound words	Fill in vocabulary in context from illustrations with a partner	Contribute vocabulary or match to illustrated word charts, games, or other materials with a partner	Use vocabulary to design visually supported games, word walls, puzzles, or patterns with a partner	Produce visually supported prose or lyrics from vocabulary banks or resources with a partner	Create original prose or lyrics from vocabulary resources (e.g., computer tools)

NATIVE LANGUAGES & CULTURES

Standard 3

English language learners **communicate** information, ideas, and concepts necessary for academic success in the area of MATHEMATICS

Domain	Topic	Level 1	Level 2	Level 3	Level 4	Level 5
LISTENING	Time (digital and analog)	Draw or show on clocks responses to oral directions (e.g., "Put the big hand on the 5.")	Role-play activities associated with different times of day in response to oral statements (e.g., "I go to bed at half past 8.")	Illustrate, by drawing or using clocks, responses to oral questions or statements (e.g., "Show me a time between 6 and 9 o'clock" or "When do we eat lunch?")	Estimate elapsed amount of time from oral word problems using visual or graphic support	Make inferences from oral grade-level story problems or classroom narratives
SPEAKING	Money Whole numbers Estimation	Identify and sort (e.g., by size, value) coins and bills (from the United States and other countries) or numerals with a partner	Exchange information about prices from visually supported materials (e.g., newspapers in L1 or L2) with a partner	Simulate buying and selling merchandise using coins or bills (e.g., "What can you buy for about $75?" with a partner	Compare prices of items across stores in the United States or between the United States and other countries with a partner	Make hypothetical purchases and discuss value in the United States or other countries (e.g., "What would you buy if you had $100 and why?")

NATIVE LANGUAGES & CULTURES

Standard 3

English language learners **communicate** information, ideas, and concepts necessary for academic success in the area of MATHEMATICS

Domain	Topic	Level 1	Level 2	Level 3	Level 4	Level 5
READING	Basic operations	Identify words associated with symbols for addition, subtraction, or multiplication with a partner (e.g., + goes with "and" or "plus")	Locate or sort phrases associated with symbols for addition, subtraction, or multiplication with a partner (e.g., "Twelve take away two is ten.")	Select and categorize by operation equivalent phrases or sentences in illustrated text with a partner	Arrange sentences in logical order to create illustrated story problems with a partner	Analyze extended text to find clues for problem solving (e.g., "There are six red balls *and* two green balls. How many balls are there *in all?*")
WRITING	Two-dimensional shapes	Label shapes of everyday, real-life examples	Generate lists of everyday illustrated examples of shapes (e.g., rectangles: windows, doors, books)	Describe features of everyday illustrated examples of shapes (e.g., "A door has four sides.")	Create descriptive paragraphs using features from everyday illustrated examples of shapes	Produce stories using features from everyday examples of shapes

NATIVE LANGUAGES & CULTURES

Standard 4
English language learners **communicate** information, ideas, and concepts necessary for academic success in the area of SCIENCE

Domain	Topic	Level 1	Level 2	Level 3	Level 4	Level 5
LISTENING	Astronomy	Draw or identify objects in the sky from models and pictures according to oral directions (e.g., "The sun is a round, yellow ball.")	Draw and position objects in the sky from models or maps according to oral directions (e.g., "Draw the sun in the middle of the page.")	Locate objects in the sky from videos or maps according to oral descriptions (e.g., "Pluto looks small because it is the farthest planet from the sun.")	Differentiate among objects in the sky (e.g., constellations, meteors, comets) from videos or maps according to oral descriptions	Define relationships among objects in the sky (e.g., eclipse or equinox) from oral descriptions
SPEAKING	Motion	Locate and name materials and supplies for investigating familiar moving objects (soccer ball, tennis ball) with a partner	State uses for materials and supplies for investigating moving objects with a partner	Outline steps for investigating moving objects with a partner	Monitor steps while investigating moving objects, and discuss results with a partner	Explain meaning and implications of results of investigating moving objects with a partner

NATIVE LANGUAGES & CULTURES

English language learners **communicate** information, ideas, and concepts
necessary for academic success in the area of SCIENCE

Domain	Topic	Level 1	Level 2	Level 3	Level 4	Level 5
READING	Life cycles Water cycle Organisms and environments	Match pictures with labels (e.g., tadpoles/frogs, caterpillars/ butterflies)	Sequence phases of cycles or associate pictures with phases using graphic support	Draw or select responses to visually or graphically supported descriptive paragraphs about phases or stages in cycles	Categorize extended text according to illustrated phases or stages of processes (e.g., in the food chain)	Compare information about various cycles or organisms and apply analysis to new contexts
WRITING	Plants Animals	Draw and label local plant or animal species from real-life observations, experiences, or pictures	Draw and describe physical attributes of local plant or animal species from real-life observations, experiences, or pictures	Compare physical attributes of local plant or animal species from real-life observations, experiences, or pictures, using graphic support	Rewrite notes on or comparisons of local plant or animal species from real-life observations or experiences to produce sentences or paragraphs	Maintain journals or learning logs describing local plant or animal species and environments based on real-life observations or experiences

NATIVE LANGUAGES & CULTURES

Grade Level 1–3

Standard 5

English language learners **communicate** information, ideas, and concepts necessary for academic success in the area of SOCIAL STUDIES

Domain	Topic	Level 1	Level 2	Level 3	Level 4	Level 5
LISTENING	Land forms Globes Maps	Mark or point to major physical features according to color or other attributes from oral commands (e.g., "Find the oceans; they are blue.")	Visualize and point to physical features or places from different perspectives, following oral commands (e.g., "Find your state on the map and globe.")	Follow directions to locate places described orally using legends, icons, or the compass rose	Interpret representations of major physical features from oral statements (e.g., "Show me the most mountainous region.")	Build models from examples based on a set of oral directions
SPEAKING	Communities Local governments Cultural heritage	Identify landmarks or people from pictures or field trips	Describe national identities, customs, or traditions using visual support (e.g., flags)	Relate aspects of local or cultural histories to a partner using artifacts or other realia	Compare aspects of local or cultural histories using visual support (e.g., multicultural picture books)	Interview persons, summarize, and report historical or cultural information from local sources

NATIVE LANGUAGES & CULTURES

Standard 5

English language learners **communicate** information, ideas, and concepts necessary for academic success in the area of SOCIAL STUDIES

Domain	Topic	Level 1	Level 2	Level 3	Level 4	Level 5
READING	Time and chronology	Sort events or historical figures from then and now using visual support	Categorize events or historical figures in the past, present, or future using visual and graphic support	Sequence events or historical figures using graphic support (e.g., time lines)	Link events, figures, or ideas in relational terms portraying historical perspectives (e.g., years, decades, or centuries) using graphic support	Interpret how historical figures, events, and ideas have changed over time from modified grade-level materials
WRITING	Needs of groups, societies, and cultures	Label coins or illustrated representations of global economies with a partner	Draw and list ways in which people use money, supported by realia or other visuals, and share in small groups	Describe personal ways to earn, spend, and save money, and share in small groups	Explain and give examples of how families around the world use money, and share in small groups	Compare how families or businesses around the world need and use money (e.g., in narrative or expository genres)

NATIVE LANGUAGES & CULTURES

Standard 1

English language learners **communicate** for SOCIAL, INTERCULTURAL, and INSTRUCTIONAL purposes within the school setting

Domain	Topic	Level 1	Level 2	Level 3	Level 4	Level 5
LISTENING	Body language/ gestures	Attend to and respond to nonverbal cues in small groups	Show examples of nonverbal behavior common to own and new cultures in small groups	Share examples of nonverbal behavior from different cultures through role play	Compare examples of nonverbal behavior across cultures through role play	Express cross-cultural communication through nonverbal behavior
SPEAKING	Tone Volume Stress Intonation Register	Repeat phrases according to audience or situation	Respond to formulaic questions and statements according to audience or situation	Begin to use speech patterns according to audience and situation (e.g., in addressing peers, adults)	Adjust speech, when reminded by adults, according to audience and situation	Vary speech patterns appropriate to audience and situation

NATIVE LANGUAGES & CULTURES

Standard 1

English language learners **communicate** for SOCIAL, INTERCULTURAL, and INSTRUCTIONAL purposes within the school setting

Domain	Topic	Level 1	Level 2	Level 3	Level 4	Level 5
READING	Strategies	Use illustrations to decipher words or phrases in small groups	Use context and illustrations at the sentence level in small groups	Use punctuation and cohesion markers in visually supported, paragraph-level text when reading to a partner	Use self-monitoring and self-correction in contextualized discourse when reading to a partner	Make inferences from cues in decontextualized text
WRITING	Interests Opinions Preferences Wishes	List or draw preferred everyday activities from illustrations or visually supported print	Describe favorite activities, games, foods, or music from illustrations, ads, or demonstrations	Recommend activities, games, books, movies, food, or music from ads or real-life examples	Make choices and provide reasons for selection of activities, games, books, movies, food, or music	Evaluate pros and cons for choosing activities, games, books, movies, food, or music, and justify selection

NATIVE LANGUAGES & CULTURES

Grade Level 4–5

Standard 2

English language learners **communicate** information, ideas, and concepts necessary for academic success in the area of LANGUAGE ARTS

Domain	Topic	Level 1	Level 2	Level 3	Level 4	Level 5
LISTENING	Strategies Phonemes/ phonology	Point at graphic representations of sounds (e.g., letter combinations) in response to teachers' reading of illustrated multicultural stories	Follow directions (e.g., sorting long vowel sounds) in response to teachers' reading of illustrated multicultural stories	Respond nonverbally (e.g., thumbs-up, thumbs-down) for rhyming words or affixes during shared reading of illustrated multicultural text	Identify targeted vocabulary nonverbally (e.g., pointing out cognates) during guided reading of visually supported multicultural text	Role-play reading of multicultural, grade-level text (e.g., in literature circles)
SPEAKING	Point of view	Describe self with words and gestures, using visual support	Compare physical traits of self or others with pictures of familiar persons	Compare physical traits of self with graphic depictions of characters in familiar fiction	Compare/contrast character traits or points of view of self with those of characters in fiction	Explain differences in character traits or points of view in characters portrayed in fiction

NATIVE LANGUAGES & CULTURES

Standard 2

English language learners **communicate** information, ideas, and concepts necessary for academic success in the area of LANGUAGE ARTS

Domain	Topic	Level 1	Level 2	Level 3	Level 4	Level 5
READING	Affixes Root words Text structure and organization	Follow/point out repetitive word patterns from leveled, illustrated books or magazines	Identify sentence patterns from leveled books, illustrated trade books, or magazines	Sort illustrated narrative and expository materials according to discourse features (e.g., "once upon a time")	Interpret or evaluate illustrated narrative and expository materials according to discourse features	Compare discourse features from modified grade-level narrative and expository text
WRITING	Main ideas and details	Produce word lists of personal preferences from visual or graphic sources (e.g., picture dictionaries)	Create memos or notes on topics of personal interest from models of writing	Design short, personal writings with thesis statements from models of writing	Develop personal pieces of writing with themes and elaboration in collaboration with peers	Edit and revise personal pieces of writing for various purposes and audiences

NATIVE LANGUAGES & CULTURES

Standard 3

English language learners **communicate** information, ideas, and concepts necessary for academic success in the area of MATHEMATICS

Domain	Topic	Level 1	Level 2	Level 3	Level 4	Level 5
LISTENING	Patterns Relations Functions	Identify algebraic symbols or elements from oral commands with visual support	Match phrases to algebraic symbols or elements from visually supported oral statements	Find relationships between algebraic symbols or functions according to oral descriptions with visual support	Sort algebraic math sentences according to oral descriptions with graphic support	Analyze change and identify transformation in various contexts from oral descriptions (e.g., predicting results of increase or decrease)
SPEAKING	Basic operations (addition, subtraction, multiplication, division)	State and confirm operation, represented visually, with a partner (in L1)	Relate how to solve problems from models with a partner (e.g., "I need to put groups together.")	Use sequential language to outline steps to solve everyday problems, and share with a partner	Give everyday, descriptive examples of how to solve problems with a partner or in small groups	Explain how to use information from solving problems in everyday situations

NATIVE LANGUAGES & CULTURES

Standard 3

English language learners **communicate** information, ideas, and concepts necessary for academic success in the area of MATHEMATICS

Domain	Topic	Level 1	Level 2	Level 3	Level 4	Level 5
READING	Three-dimensional shapes Polygons Angles	Sort figures by characteristics and properties from labeled visuals or objects (e.g., three sides, four angles)	Match characteristics and properties from visuals, objects, and phrases (e.g., the corner or right angle of the square)	Distinguish among figures from visually supported descriptions	Construct or draw figures by following steps of visually supported text	Infer geometric relationships among figures from modified grade-level text
WRITING	Data analysis	Label variables or sets from graphs, tables, or charts working with a partner	Formulate and answer *wh-* questions from graphs, tables, or charts working with a partner	Organize, display, and describe information in graphs, tables, or charts with a partner	Produce paragraphs using information from graphs, tables, or charts	Summarize and apply information in graphs, tables, or charts to new situations

NATIVE LANGUAGES & CULTURES

Grade Level 4–5

Standard 4

English language learners **communicate** information, ideas, and concepts necessary for academic success in the area of SCIENCE

Domain	Topic	Level 1	Level 2	Level 3	Level 4	Level 5
LISTENING	Health Body systems Living systems	Match words with labels on diagrams or models based on oral commands	Select examples of body parts from magazines, models, or other visuals based on oral directions (e.g., "Find a skull.")	Create displays of body parts, organs, or systems using visuals based on oral descriptions	Organize information about various organs or systems from visually supported teacher explanations	Evaluate hypothetical oral scenarios involving information about organs or systems (e.g., "Which organ would be most useful when ...?")
SPEAKING	Earth's materials Natural resources	Name common natural phenomena from collections or pictures	Describe natural phenomena from collections or pictures (e.g., seashells or sponges)	Identify features of natural phenomena from collections or pictures (e.g., size or color of stones vs. rocks)	Discuss and give examples of uses of natural phenomena from collections or pictures	Explain relationships among natural phenomena using extended discourse

NATIVE LANGUAGES & CULTURES

Standard 4

English language learners **communicate** information, ideas, and concepts necessary for academic success in the area of SCIENCE

Domain	Topic	Level 1	Level 2	Level 3	Level 4	Level 5
READING	Properties of matter Energy sources	Find examples of forms of energy from billboards, magazines, and newspapers	Sequence steps of energy use and depletion from phrases and illustrations	Follow illustrated directions to test hypotheses about energy in scientific inquiry	Interpret results of inquiry from illustrated text (e.g., in lab reports)	Infer applications of information about energy gathered from modified grade-level text or inquiry-based projects
WRITING	Solar system Earth's history	Replicate labeled representations or models of the planets or solar system	Make notes from observations from videos or illustrations	Compare features from models, videos, or illustrations using graphic organizers	Maintain illustrated records, logs, or journals of features, events, or observations	Explain the physical world with examples of features, events, or observations

NATIVE LANGUAGES & CULTURES

Standard 5

English language learners **communicate** information, ideas, and concepts
necessary for academic success in the area of SOCIAL STUDIES

Domain	Topic	Level 1	Level 2	Level 3	Level 4	Level 5
LISTENING	Prehistoric animals Tools	Identify artifacts or creatures of the past in pictures and illustrations from oral descriptions	Match artifacts or creatures of the past with their environments from oral descriptions in videos or movies	Place artifacts or creatures presented in oral readings in chronological order using pictures or time lines	Reenact scenes from the past involving artifacts or creatures based on videos, movies, or oral readings	Interpret videos, movies, or oral readings about the work of paleontologists and anthropologists through role play
SPEAKING	Legends, scales, maps, globes U.S. regions Topography	State directions or locations using realia or gestures with guidance from peers	Identify features of places (e.g., "Chicago is on Lake Michigan.") using realia in small groups	Locate and describe places using realia through interaction with peers (e.g., two-way tasks)	Explore and compare locations of places using realia and other resources (e.g., the Internet) in cooperative groups	Give presentations about places using visual support (e.g., computer slide shows) in cooperative groups

NATIVE LANGUAGES & CULTURES

Standard 5

English language learners **communicate** information, ideas, and concepts necessary for academic success in the area of SOCIAL STUDIES

Domain	Topic	Level 1	Level 2	Level 3	Level 4	Level 5
READING	Explorers Historical leaders	Match time frames, places, or events to people using charts or illustrations	Associate traits, cultures, or contributions of people using graphic organizers or illustrations	Analyze traits, cultures, and contributions of people using graphic organizers or illustrations	Summarize information about people and their contributions from multiple illustrated sources	Draw conclusions about people and their contributions based on multiple, modified grade-level sources
WRITING	Immigration Colonization Cross-cultural experiences	List family members or historical figures with countries of origin, using maps or charts	Create personal or historical family trees using graphic organizers and photographs	Produce illustrated family or group histories through albums, journals, diaries, or travelogues	Research (e.g., by conducting interviews) and report family or historical journeys	Discuss, in paragraph form, cause/effect, historical patterns, or impact of movement of peoples from nation to nation

NATIVE LANGUAGES & CULTURES

Standard 1

English language learners **communicate** for SOCIAL, INTERCULTURAL, and INSTRUCTIONAL purposes within the school setting

Domain	Topic	Level 1	Level 2	Level 3	Level 4	Level 5
LISTENING	School behaviors or activities	Follow one-step oral commands supported by visuals or gestures	Follow multistep oral directions supported by visuals or gestures	Role-play situations in small groups based on dialogues, video clips, or field trips	Simulate scenarios in small groups based on broadcasts or multimedia presentations	Create or enact skits or short plays based on videos, assemblies, or multimedia presentations
SPEAKING	School life Social interaction	Respond to and offer formulaic greetings, introductions, compliments, and farewells with peers or family members	Ask and answer questions to exchange information with peers or family members	Initiate or engage in conversations with peers or in small groups (e.g., "Please tell me tonight's homework.")	Respond to or engage in conversations involving nuances, idiomatic expressions, or slang	Express or respond to humor or sarcasm in conversations (e.g., "Sure I plan to study all weekend.")

NATIVE LANGUAGES & CULTURES

Standard 1

English language learners **communicate** for SOCIAL, INTERCULTURAL, and INSTRUCTIONAL purposes within the school setting

Domain	Topic	Level 1	Level 2	Level 3	Level 4	Level 5
READING	Information gathering at school or at home Multi-culturalism	Search for and identify topics of personal interest using illustrations (from L1, Internet, or newspapers)	Indicate preferences by rank-ordering or classifying illustrated topics of personal interest	Gather and sort illustrated information according to topics of interest or diverse perspectives	Arrange illustrated information from multiple, diverse sources in logical order	Create original displays of information (e.g., posters, graphic organizers, brochures) from multiple, diverse sources
WRITING	Negotiating solutions to problems Interpersonal or cultural misunder-standings	Identify examples of common cultural misunderstandings among family and friends from videos or class discussions (in L1) with a partner	List examples of common cultural misunderstandings (e.g., chores or responsibilities) using visual or graphic support	Create descriptions or narrations of issues or cultural misunderstandings using visual or graphic support	Provide advice, rephrase, or offer possible solutions for cultural misunderstandings using visual models of writing (e.g., in newspapers)	Create guidelines for a group, class, or school on conflict resolution

NATIVE LANGUAGES & CULTURES

Standard 2

English language learners **communicate** information, ideas, and concepts necessary for academic success in the area of LANGUAGE ARTS

Domain	Topic	Level 1	Level 2	Level 3	Level 4	Level 5
LISTENING	Synonyms Antonyms Metaphors Similes	Find words that are the same or opposite (e.g., "big-huge," "night-day") represented by objects or illustrations according to oral directions	Match oral phrases involving figures of speech or vocabulary with visual representation (e.g., "as big as a house")	Identify figures of speech or vocabulary within visually supported oral discourse	Role-play scenes involving figures of speech or vocabulary based on oral descriptions (e.g., "The room was like an oven.")	Respond nonverbally to demonstrate comprehension of figures of speech and vocabulary embedded in oral discourse appropriate for grade level
SPEAKING	Multiple meanings	Identify common words represented by objects or illustrations (e.g., table, cell phone)	Produce phrases or sentences with common words represented by objects or illustrations in two contexts (e.g., "table of contents" and "times table")	Give examples of words or phrases represented by objects or illustrations in multiple contexts (e.g., "base price," "first base," "base of a triangle")	Explain differences in use of words or phrases with multiple meanings in varied contexts	Create and present scenarios that incorporate the use of words or phrases with multiple meanings

NATIVE LANGUAGES & CULTURES

Standard 2

English language learners **communicate** information, ideas, and concepts necessary for academic success in the area of LANGUAGE ARTS

Domain	Topic	Level 1	Level 2	Level 3	Level 4	Level 5
READING	Comprehension strategies Technical texts	Match objects or diagrams with written labels with a partner to construct meaning	Use headings, bold print, diagrams, and charts with a partner to construct meaning	Use context clues within graphically and visually supported text with a partner to construct meaning	Use an array of strategies with visually supported text with a partner to infer meaning	Apply reading strategies to modified grade-level text to infer and validate meaning
WRITING	Use of resources Editing Multimedia	Produce words or phrases using bilingual or picture dictionaries	Check language structures, conventions, or spelling using computers, peers, or models	Peer edit and revise drafts using checklists, models, or other resources	Self-edit and revise drafts using teacher feedback or other resources (e.g., thesauruses or reference books)	Self-assess drafts and produce final products using rubrics, guides, or other resources

NATIVE LANGUAGES & CULTURES

Grade Level 6–8

Standard 3

English language learners **communicate** information, ideas, and concepts necessary for academic success in the area of MATHEMATICS

Domain	Topic	Level 1	Level 2	Level 3	Level 4	Level 5
LISTENING	Statistics Metric units Measures of central tendency	Identify tools and units of measurement as described orally with visual depictions	Compare or classify tools and units of measurement as described orally with visual support	Draw or construct graphs and diagrams from oral descriptions using various tools and units of measurement (e.g., to illustrate *mean or mode*)	Analyze and apply use of graphic representations from oral explanations of problems or situations	Evaluate and use different representations for solving grade-level oral problems
SPEAKING	Area Volume Three-dimensional shapes	Name figures or dimensions from real objects or diagrams	Define dimensions of figures based on objects or diagrams using general language (e.g., "Height goes up and down.")	Describe dimensions of objects or diagrams using some specialized language (e.g., "You times base by height.")	Analyze figures or operations in real-life situations using specialized language (e.g., "You multiply base by height of walls to know how much paint you need.")	Explain differences in usage among operations and figures using specialized or technical language

NATIVE LANGUAGES & CULTURES

Standard 3

English language learners **communicate** information, ideas, and concepts necessary for academic success in the area of MATHEMATICS

Domain	Topic	Level 1	Level 2	Level 3	Level 4	Level 5
READING	Data sets Plots Data interpretation	Identify variables or integers presented in charts and graphs with a partner	Answer questions related to variables or integers presented in charts and graphs with a partner	Construct data sets from variables presented in text, charts, graphs, and plots with a partner	Chart, graph, or plot data sets according to written directions with a partner	Interpret data presented in charts, graphs, or plots from modified grade-level material
WRITING	Probability Ratio	Record outcomes of hands-on activities (e.g., with tallies)	Estimate outcomes with illustrations and phrases using real objects	Describe in phrases or simple sentences how to formulate estimates using concrete examples	Compare possible combinations or configurations using graphic organizers and sentences	Explain and justify use of different combinations or configurations in paragraph form

NATIVE LANGUAGES & CULTURES

Grade Level 6-8

Standard 4

English language learners **communicate** information, ideas, and concepts necessary for academic success in the area of SCIENCE

Domain	Topic	Level 1	Level 2	Level 3	Level 4	Level 5
LISTENING	Atoms Cells Molecules	Identify elements within models or diagrams according to oral directions	Match oral descriptions of functions of various elements with models or diagrams	Arrange models or diagrams based on sequential oral directions (e.g., stages of mitosis or fission)	Reproduce models or diagrams based on visually supported tapes, CDs, videos, or lectures	Design or construct models or diagrams from decontextualized oral discourse
SPEAKING	Solar system	Repeat definitions of key objects in the solar system (e.g., planets, asteroids) with a partner	Describe appearance and composition of objects in the solar system with a partner	Compare appearance and composition of objects in the galaxy with a partner	Present or discuss illustrated processes involving planetary objects (e.g., measuring distances or time spans)	Explain, using technical terms, the structure of the universe using examples of planetary components (e.g., stars and galaxies)

NATIVE LANGUAGES & CULTURES

Standard 4

English language learners **communicate** information, ideas, and concepts necessary for academic success in the area of SCIENCE

Domain	Topic	Level 1	Level 2	Level 3	Level 4	Level 5
READING	Body systems Organs	Match descriptive phrases or words to diagrams or models	Classify short descriptions of systems (e.g., respiratory or digestive) using visual or graphic support	Find or sort visually or graphically supported information about processes (e.g., veins vs. arteries)	Transform graphically supported, expository text into sequenced steps to illustrate processes (e.g., oxygen exchange)	Make predictions or inferences (e.g., consequences of losing kidney function) from modified grade-level material
WRITING	Weather Climate zones Natural disasters	Draw and label charts of features, conditions, or occurrences using information from newspapers or the Internet	Describe features, conditions, or occurrences around the world based on newspapers, the Internet, or illustrated text	Compare features, conditions, or occurrences between two areas (e.g., native country and the United States) using information from multiple sources	Narrate personal impact of features, conditions, or occurrences around the world using multiple sources (e.g., the Internet and family stories)	Interpret global impact of varying features, conditions, or occurrences from modified grade-level source material

NATIVE LANGUAGES & CULTURES

Grade Level 6–8

Standard 5

English language learners **communicate** information, ideas, and concepts necessary for academic success in the area of SOCIAL STUDIES

Domain	Topic	Level 1	Level 2	Level 3	Level 4	Level 5
LISTENING	Maps Longitude Latitude Time zones	Find individual features or locations named orally on maps with a partner	Classify features or locations on maps (e.g., places in the Northern or Southern Hemisphere) from oral statements with a partner	Identify features or locations on maps from a series of oral statements with a partner (e.g., in two-way tasks)	Match oral descriptions of features or locations on maps with a partner	Sequence detailed descriptions of features or locations according to oral travelogues
SPEAKING	Rights and responsibilities Freedom and democracy Slavery	Respond to questions with words or phrases related to illustrated historical scenes	Make general statements about illustrated historical scenes (e.g., "Women do vote now. Women did not vote in 1900.")	Describe or enact historical scenarios based on illustrations or historical cartoons	State a stance or position using conditional language (e.g., "If I lived in the 1850s …") from visually supported historical scenarios	Evaluate or imagine different historical scenarios and their impact or consequences (e.g., "Imagine if we could not vote.")

NATIVE LANGUAGES & CULTURES

Standard 5

English language learners **communicate** information, ideas, and concepts necessary for academic success in the area of SOCIAL STUDIES

Domain	Topic	Level 1	Level 2	Level 3	Level 4	Level 5
READING	Revolution Bill of Rights U.S. Constitution	Match words or phrases about actions or events with photographs or illustrations	Classify or categorize visually supported statements about actions or events by time frames (e.g., before, during, after war)	Order paragraphs describing actions or events using visual or graphic support (e.g., a time line)	Match actions or events to summaries of expanded text with some visual or graphic support	Infer or determine relationships (e.g., cause/effect) of actions or events using modified grade-level material
WRITING	Cultural perspectives and frames of reference Countries Continents Ancient/ medieval civilizations	List characteristics of people, places, or time periods using visual or graphic cultural references	Describe people, places, or time periods using visual or graphic cultural references (e.g., map of Southeast Asia or artifacts from Ming Dynasty)	Compare/contrast people, places, or time periods using visual or graphic cultural references (e.g., Aztec, Mayan, and Egyptian pyramids)	Give detailed examples of cross-cultural connections among people, places, or time periods using visual or graphic references	Defend and provide support for cross-cultural perspectives

NATIVE LANGUAGES & CULTURES

Standard 1

English language learners **communicate** for SOCIAL, INTERCULTURAL, and INSTRUCTIONAL purposes within the school setting

Domain	Topic	Level 1	Level 2	Level 3	Level 4	Level 5
LISTENING	Idiomatic expressions Slang Humor Sarcasm	Follow one-step instructions or requests supported by gestures from peers (e.g., "Wait way back there.")	Attend to and respond nonverbally to short dialogues or conversations supported by gestures from familiar speakers	Respond nonverbally to slang or idiomatic expressions, especially when interacting with peers (e.g., through facial expressions or actions)	Respond to nuances elicited by unfamiliar speakers (after clarifying or verifying with peers)	Provide appropriate responses to nuances in a variety of contexts and situations
SPEAKING	Interpersonal issues Misunder-standings	Share potential cross-cultural misunderstandings in small groups (using L1)	Give examples of cross-cultural misunderstandings in small groups (confirming through L1)	Present and pose solutions to cross-cultural misunderstandings in small groups or with a partner	Negotiate solutions to resolve cross-cultural misunderstandings with a partner	Offer suggestions and guidance on how to reach compromise or agreement on cross-cultural misunderstandings

NATIVE LANGUAGES & CULTURES

Standard 1

Englisgh language learners **communicate** for SOCIAL, INTERCULTURAL, and INSTRUCTIONAL purposes within the school setting

Domain	Topic	Level 1	Level 2	Level 3	Level 4	Level 5
READING	Strategies	Preview visually supported text to glean basic information (e.g., menus, schedules, announcements)	Connect information from visually supported text to self and personal experiences	Scan visually or graphically supported text to obtain information	Skim visually or graphically supported text to confirm or verify information	Revise thinking or draw conclusions from information in modified grade-level text
WRITING	Advice Suggestions Recommendations	List topics of common personal interest with a classmate	Compare key points about topics of common personal interest using graphic organizers	Produce or respond to e-mails, notes, or memos from teachers or peers using appropriate register	Create or respond to everyday issues (e.g., advice columns, editorials in school or local papers) using appropriate register and language forms	Compose personal or business forms of correspondence using appropriate register and language forms (e.g., letters, applications, essays)

NATIVE LANGUAGES & CULTURES

Standard 2

English language learners **communicate** information, ideas, and concepts necessary for academic success in the area of LANGUAGE ARTS

Domain	Topic	Level 1	Level 2	Level 3	Level 4	Level 5
LISTENING	Bias Author's perspective Points of view	Identify topics or themes presented in media sources (e.g., TV, films, videos) with a partner	Differentiate fact from opinion from media sources (e.g., TV, films, videos) with a partner	Compare and contrast varying stances presented in media sources with a group	Draw conclusions about various stances from speakers using visually supported material in group projects (e.g., on prejudice)	Deduce stances by integrating information from various speakers
SPEAKING	Critical commentaries	State facts related to personal or cultural preferences using visually supported materials (e.g., in dating)	Give opinions on personal or cultural issues using realia or visual support	Offer pros and cons of issues using visual or graphic support	Discuss and summarize current critical issues using visual or graphic support	Deliver multimedia presentations on controversial topics

NATIVE LANGUAGES & CULTURES

Standard 2

English language learners **communicate** information, ideas, and concepts necessary for academic success in the area of LANGUAGE ARTS

Domain	Topic	Level 1	Level 2	Level 3	Level 4	Level 5
READING	Literary genres	Match type of genre to short descriptions (in L1 or L2) with a partner	Sort short segments of dramatic, poetic, or narrative works according to typical characteristics (in L1 or L2) with a partner	Categorize types of works from a variety of genres (in L1 or L2) with a partner	Identify the purposes and uses of particular genres with a partner	Analyze excerpts or favorite genres from modified grade-level material
WRITING	Autobiographical and biographical narratives	Label personal photographs, artifacts, or drawings with words or phrases	List life events sequentially or along a time line using phrases or short sentences	Summarize life events organized by time period using personal resources (e.g., albums, birth certificates)	Create personal essays using as models familiar autobiographies or memoirs read (in L1 or L2)	Compose autobiographical essays or memoirs

NATIVE LANGUAGES & CULTURES

Grade Level 9–12

Standard 3

English language learners **communicate** information, ideas, and concepts necessary for academic success in the area of MATHEMATICS

Domain	Topic	Level 1	Level 2	Level 3	Level 4	Level 5
LISTENING	Quadrilaterals	Identify properties of figures (e.g., opposite sides or angles) in small groups based on visual representations and oral statements	Compare or classify examples of figures with a partner based on visual representations and oral descriptions	Draw or construct figures using materials or computer software with a partner based on oral directions	Respond (through pointing or drawing) to language associated with deductive proofs involving sides and angles of figures with a partner	Follow oral directions to generate transformations of geometric shapes using materials or computer software, and grade-level text
SPEAKING	Problem solving	State or repeat steps in problem solving using manipulatives or visual support	Describe steps in solving problems using tools or technology (e.g., protractors, calculators)	Explain steps used in problem solving assisted by mental math or think-alouds	Present two or more approaches to solving the same math problem as part of a team presentation	Discuss and provide examples of a variety of strategies for solving grade-level math problems

NATIVE LANGUAGES & CULTURES

English language learners **communicate** information, ideas, and concepts necessary for academic success in the area of MATHEMATICS

Domain	Topic	Level 1	Level 2	Level 3	Level 4	Level 5
READING	Data displays Data interpretation	Match data in graphic representations from everyday sources (e.g., newspapers, magazines) to text with a partner	Sort and rank, with a partner, information gathered from data on graphs (e.g., stock quotes, sports statistics)	Analyze comparative language to draw conclusions from data in charts, tables, and graphs with a partner	Organize, display, and interpret data from visually or graphically supported material with a partner	Make predictions based on charts and graphs from modified grade-level text
WRITING	Algebra	Copy and label equations, inequalities, or expressions from overheads or models	Describe simple equations, inequalities, or expressions from real-life situations with a partner	Create explanations for equations, inequalities, or expressions with a partner	Provide justifications (e.g., proofs) to solutions of equations, inequalities, or expressions in small groups	Compose word problems that fit equations, inequalities, or expressions

NATIVE LANGUAGES & CULTURES

Grade Level 9–12

Standard 4

English language learners **communicate** information, ideas, and concepts necessary for academic success in the area of SCIENCE

Domain	Topic	Level 1	Level 2	Level 3	Level 4	Level 5
LISTENING	Nuclear structures and functions	Distinguish parts of elements (e.g., atoms, molecules) from oral statements using visuals, models, or manipulatives	Compare the arrangement of elements (e.g., atoms, ionic crystals, polymers) from oral statements using visual or graphic support	Draw or build models of elements from oral descriptions in small groups	Create representations of the properties, features, and uses of elements from oral descriptions in small groups	Evaluate delivery of oral reports about elements presented by peers
SPEAKING	Chemical or physical change Compounds	Name and describe common mixtures and compounds, and their composition, from visuals, real-life examples, or symbols (e.g., H_2O)	State or predict transformations or exchanges involving chemical or physical reactions with a partner	Outline steps, using sequential language, in transformations or exchanges involving chemical or physical reactions with a partner	Report and exchange information on processes and results from chemical or physical reactions with a partner	Explain changes in matter, the nature of changes, and their real-world applications in extended discourse

NATIVE LANGUAGES & CULTURES

Standard 4

English language learners **communicate** information, ideas, and concepts necessary for academic success in the area of SCIENCE

Domain	Topic	Level 1	Level 2	Level 3	Level 4	Level 5
READING	Scientific research and investigation	Match vocabulary associated with scientific inquiry with illustrated examples	Categorize phrases and sentences descriptive of processes and products of scientific inquiry using graphic support (e.g., hypotheses, variables, results)	Sequence paragraphs descriptive of the processes and products of scientific inquiry using graphic support	Extract information on the processes and products of scientific inquiry using graphic support (e.g., lab reports)	Analyze, review, and critique explanations and conclusions from scientific inquiry using modified grade-level materials
WRITING	Conservation of energy and matter	Label or list everyday ways to preserve or protect the environment using real-life examples or other visual support	Describe with examples how to preserve or protect the environment using graphic support	Compare results of experiments or readings on ecology (e.g., biodegradability of materials) using visual or graphic support	Summarize experiments, readings, or research on ecology using visual or graphic support	Select and defend ecological methods and explain their real-world applications

NATIVE LANGUAGES & CULTURES

Standard 5

English language learners **communicate** information, ideas, and concepts necessary for academic success in the area of SOCIAL STUDIES

Domain	Topic	Level 1	Level 2	Level 3	Level 4	Level 5
LISTENING	Supreme Court cases Federal, civil, and individual rights Social issues and inequities	Find basic information in photographs or illustrations as described in oral statements (e.g., dates, people, or titles in newspapers or magazines)	Identify topics or political issues in photographs or illustrations based on oral descriptions	Compare oral summaries of political situations with visual representations (e.g., video of Dr. Martin Luther King's "I Have a Dream" speech)	Interpret peers' reenactments of or presentations on political situations as seen in the media	Evaluate mock trials or political speeches by peers
SPEAKING	Human populations	Exchange facts about the peoples, languages, or cultures of local communities or native countries with a partner (using L1 or L2)	Share personal experiences and reactions to migration/immigration with a partner	Discuss demographic shifts, migration/immigration patterns, languages or cultures in small groups	Explain the impact of demographic shifts or migration/immigration patterns on peoples, languages, or cultures in small groups	Give multimedia demonstrations, speeches, or presentations on characteristics, distribution, and migration of peoples, their languages, and their cultures

NATIVE LANGUAGES & CULTURES

Standard 5

English language learners **communicate** information, ideas, and concepts necessary for academic success in the area of SOCIAL STUDIES

Domain	Topic	Level 1	Level 2	Level 3	Level 4	Level 5
READING	Global economy Supply and demand Money and banking	Make connections between areas on maps or globes and their products or monetary units using illustrated sources	Glean information about places, products, or monetary units from newspapers, charts, and graphs	Detect trends or fluctuations in monetary values or production from summaries and information presented in charts, tables, and graphs	Predict future trends in monetary values or production presented in graphically supported text	Interpret economic trends based on modified grade-level materials (e.g., business reports, magazine articles)
WRITING	Cultural diversity and cohesion International and multinational organizations	Brainstorm and record examples of multicultural institutions, or symbols (e.g., the Red Cross) in small groups	List and define multicultural issues, institutions, or symbols in small groups	Compare what "is" to what "should be" in regard to multicultural issues or institutions using graphic organizers	State and defend a stance or position on multicultural issues or institutions using feedback from a peer	Produce essays, poems, or brochures that address or pose creative solutions to multicultural issues

NATIVE LANGUAGES & CULTURES

Ways to Implement the Standards

Ways to Implement
the Standards

This section provides a preliminary discussion of ways educators can implement the English language proficiency standards by

- planning instruction and assessment
- transforming the elements of a sample performance indicator
- collaborating with other educators

Planning Instruction and Assessment

The English language proficiency standards are broad statements encompassing the range of language competencies required of all English language learners for success in the classroom. Within language domains, defining the modality in which the standards are employed, the strands of sample performance indicators offer concrete examples of how the standards may be translated into teaching practice.

Thus, to design standards-based instruction and assessment for English language learners, we turn to the sample performance indicators, as they are the closest representations of what occurs in classrooms. A strand of sample performance indicators illustrates student performance at varying levels of English language proficiency in response to specific learning tasks.

The language, content, and support or strategy that constitute the sample performance indicators are starting points for designing specific lesson plans for English language learners to develop their language proficiency and content mastery (see Figure 12). Student performance stems from the interaction among these elements, which are common to all sample performance indicators. As shown in Figure 13, teachers need to consider all three elements when planning lessons or units for students at differing levels of language proficiency.

Using the Strands of Model Performance Indicators

The abbreviated lesson shown in Figure 14 is designed to teach students in Grade 3 about the topic of scientific inquiry. The students in the class are at Developing to Bridging levels of English language proficiency (from Levels 3 through 5), perhaps mixed with proficient English speakers. For this lesson, the teacher is concentrating on helping students develop their speaking skills. The teacher thinks about what students will need to do and includes *language*, *content*, and *support* in the lesson plan.

As part of the plan, the teacher uses ongoing assessment to check on the students' progress toward attaining Standard 4. To assess language, the teacher uses a checklist containing the

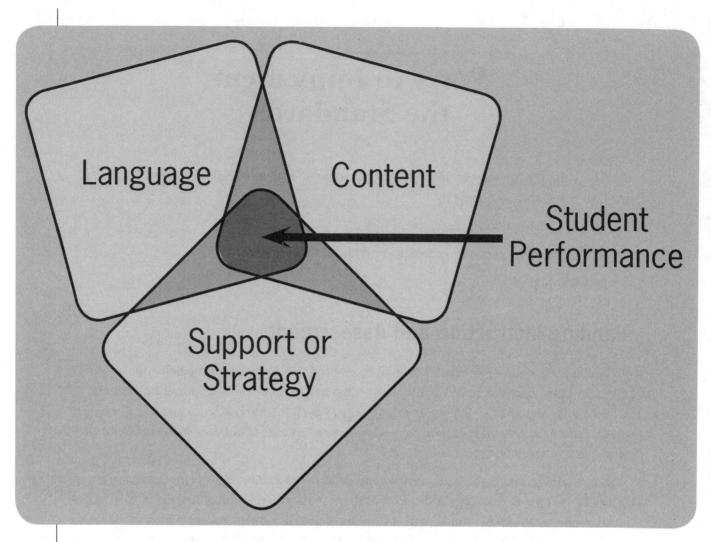

Figure 12. General Model for Planning Instruction and Assessment Using the Elements Drawn From Sample Performance Indicators

language objectives. As students work in pairs or small groups, the teacher observes them, noting whether they use the targeted scientific language, the enumerators, and the questioning techniques for clarification with their partners or with the teacher. To assess content, the teacher puts a chart listing the steps of the scientific inquiry on an overhead projector. That way, partners can check each other's work to see if they have included all the steps.

Standard 5: The language of social studies
Grade-level cluster: 4–5
Language domain: Listening
Topic: Prehistoric animals and tools
Language proficiency level: 1 (Starting)
Sample performance indicator: Identify artifacts or creatures of the past in pictures and illustrations from oral descriptions.

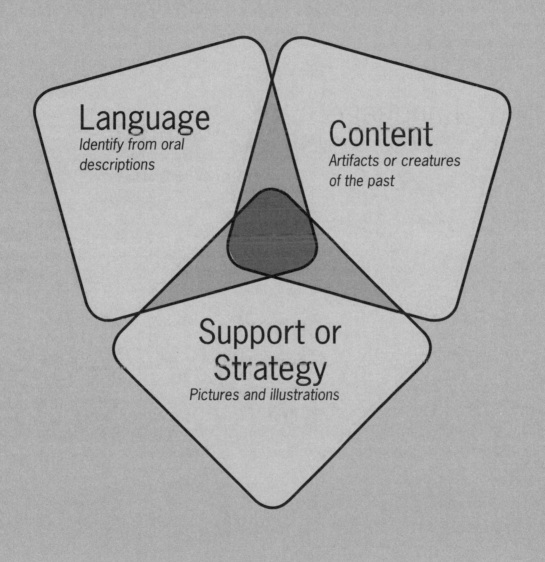

Language
Identify from oral descriptions

Content
Artifacts or creatures of the past

Support or Strategy
Pictures and illustrations

Figure 13. Specific Models for Planning Instruction and Assessment Drawn From Sample Performance Indicators

Standard 1: Language for social, intercultural, and instructional purposes
Grade-level cluster: 9–12
Language domain: Speaking
Topic: Interpersonal issues and misunderstandings
Language proficiency level: 3 (Developing)
Sample performance indicator: Present and pose solutions to cross-cultural misunderstandings in small groups or with a partner

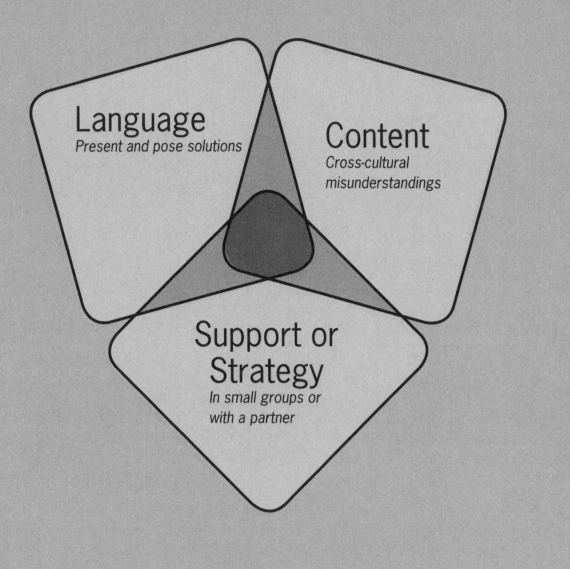

Figure 13 (continued). Specific Models for Planning Instruction and Assessment Drawn From Sample Performance Indicators

Standard 4: The language of science
Grade-level cluster: 1–3
Language domain: Speaking
Topic: Motion

English language proficiency levels		
3 **Expanding**	**4** **Developing**	**5** **Bridging**
Outline steps for investigating moving objects with a partner	Monitor steps while investigating moving objects, and discuss results with a partner	Explain meaning and implications of results of investigating moving objects with a partner

Content Objective

• Conduct scientific inquiry while following prescribed steps

To meet the content objective, the students will list verbally the steps in scientific inquiry (develop a hypothesis, design an experiment, collect data, analyze data, and draw conclusions to test the hypothesis).

Language Objectives

• Practice using the vocabulary of scientific inquiry, minimally at the sentence level

• Incorporate enumerators into speech

• Formulate questions

To meet the language objectives, the students will use

• vocabulary of scientific inquiry: *thesis, hypothesis, analyze, conclusion, predict, experiment*

• enumerators: *first, second, third, . . .* or *The first step is . . ., The second step is . . .*

• questioning techniques for clarification: *Do you mean . . .? How do you say this word (hypothesis) in English? Does this step come first or second?*

Support
Students may
• work with a partner or in small groups
• follow charts or graphic organizers describing scientific inquiry in a teacher presentation or outlining a previous reading in a textbook

Figure 14. A Sample Plan for Teaching Scientific Inquiry

An approach to planning instruction and assessment that integrates language, content, and support may be effective for all students; however, it is a *necessity* if English language learners are to access the material and comprehend it. As illustrated in Figure 15, when students are at the initial levels of language proficiency, they require support and strategies to help them access content. As students' proficiency grows, they are able to understand and produce language that is increasingly more complex. As a result, the need for scaffolding ebbs, though it may never disappear.

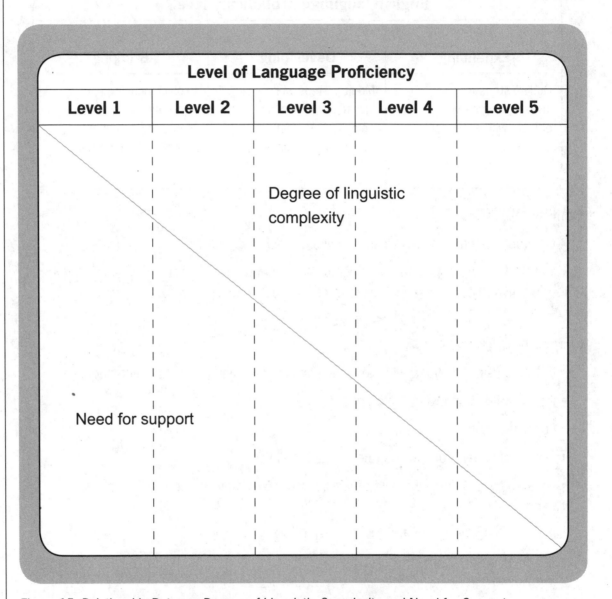

Figure 15. Relationship Between Degree of Linguistic Complexity and Need for Support

Transforming the Elements of a Sample Performance Indicator

The sample performance indicators exemplify how standards are realized in the classroom. As samples, they do not represent the full range of curriculum and instruction across grade levels, content areas, and state or district frameworks. The flexibility of the sample performance indicators enables teachers to shape instruction for their individual classrooms. *Transformations* provide a process to help teachers and other educators adapt the sample performance indicators to meet the particular language needs of English language learners.

Transformations entail changing one or more of the elements making up a sample performance indicator—language function, content, or support/strategy—to reflect local instructional targets more closely. Another possible transformation is a change in language domain.

In many cases, the sample performance indicators are written in general terms. For example, the sample performance indicator in Standard 2, reading, for grade-level cluster 9–12 states, "Identify the purposes and uses of particular genres with a partner." Teachers may insert any genre that applies to the grade-level cluster (see the list of topics in Appendix D). Thus, the content can become specific to the context of study, such as "Identify the purposes and uses of *critical commentary* with a partner" or "Identify the purposes and uses of *biographical narratives* with a partner."

In other cases, sample performance indicators are more specific. The series of transformations described below illustrates how educators can change each element of a sample performance indicator to personalize instruction and assessment.

Change in Language Function

The first transformation below represents a change in language function; the content and support remain constant. In the sample performance indicator on the left, students are being asked to explain and give details about something. In the sample performance indicator on the right, students are being asked to *develop* something. Although *explaining* and *developing* are both language functions, students use different sets of linguistic features to express themselves and to demonstrate proficiency.

Standard 1: Language for social, intercultural, and instructional purposes
Grade-level cluster: 1–3
Language domain: Writing
Language proficiency level: 4 (Expanding)

Explain and give details of special events or celebrations at school, at home, or in the home country using drawings or graphic organizers	**Language function transformation:** from *explain and give details* to *develop* →	*Develop* travel brochures or posters about special events or celebrations at school, at home, or in the home country using drawings or graphic organizers

Change in Academic Content

The next transformation represents a change in academic content; the language function and visual supports remain the same. In the sample performance indicator on the left, students are working with artifacts or creatures of the past. On the right, geographic regions has replaced that content or context.

Standard 5: The language of social studies
Grade-level cluster: 4–5
Language domain: Listening
Language proficiency level: 2 (Emerging)

Match *artifacts or creatures of the past* with their environments from oral descriptions in videos or movies	**Content transformation:** from *artifacts or creatures of the past* to *geographic regions* →	Match *geographic regions* with their environments from oral descriptions in videos and movies

Change in Support or Strategy

The third example represents a transformation in the support or strategy; the language function and academic content remain unaltered. As different types of support lend themselves to different groups of students, the same academic content can be delivered while adapting the support. In the example below, the sample performance indicator on the left uses visual support as the strategy, while the support in the sample performance indicator on the right has been transformed to an interactive one, *working in pairs or triads*.

Standard 2: The language of language arts
Grade-level cluster: 6–8
Language domain: Listening
Language proficiency level: 3 (Developing)

Identify figures of speech or vocabulary within *visually supported* oral discourse	**Support/strategy transformation:** from *visual support* to *working in pairs or triads*	Identify figures of speech or vocabulary within oral discourse *working in pairs or triads*

Change in Language Domain

The last transformation represents a change in language domain. The academic content remains constant, but the language task shifts. In the sample performance indicator on the left, the language domain of writing is reflected in the act of *copying* or *creating a list*. In the transformation on the right, the domain has shifted to oral language, speaking, as illustrated by the language functions of *presenting* or *enumerating*.

Standard 4: The language of science
Grade-level cluster: PreK–K
Language domain: Writing
Language proficiency level: 3 (Developing)

Copy or *create* a list of materials (e.g., for growing seeds) using a combination of drawings, letters, scribble writings, and words with invented spellings	**Language domain transformation:** from *writing* to *speaking* →	*Present* a list or *enumerate* materials needed to conduct scientific inquiry (e.g., for growing seeds)

Collaborating With Other Educators

Systemic educational reform requires sustained effort on the part of all teachers and administrators. ESL educators must work hand in hand with other school personnel to plan instruction, coordinate services, and advocate on behalf of English language learners. The following are suggestions for collaboration and joint effort between ESL and other educators.

Planning Between ESL and Content Teachers

- Select language proficiency and academic content standards for instruction and assessment.
- Formulate language and content objectives; decide on types of support or strategies.
- Design standards-based lessons and thematic units.
- Create instructional assessment activities and rubrics for interpreting student work.

Planning Between ESL and Bilingual Teachers

- Select language proficiency and academic content standards.
- Preview standards-based lessons in the first language; reinforce lessons in English, the second language.
- Choose complementary materials and resources in the first and second languages.
- Differentiate instruction according to students' levels of language proficiency in the first and second languages.

Planning Between ESL and Resource Teachers

- Coordinate standards-based literacy instruction in the second language (and first language).
- Share diagnostic tools and other forms of formative assessment.
- Provide detailed information on student progress.
- Offer suggestions to classroom teachers for grading.

Planning Between ESL and Classroom/Mainstream Teachers

- Participate in grade-level meetings.
- Team teach or coach, as appropriate, standards-based lessons.
- Share rubrics and other means of interpreting student work.
- Participate together in sustained professional development.

Planning Between ESL and Special Education Teachers

- Attend prereferral and individualized education planning meetings.
- Plan lessons to ensure that language needs and learning disabilities are addressed.
- Team teach or coach, as appropriate, standards-based content lessons.

- Meet with parents or family members to ensure information is disseminated in the first language.

Planning Among ESL Program, School, and District Administrators

- Design a well-articulated service delivery model for English language learners.

- Offer ongoing professional development opportunities, including workshops, graduate course work, and online training.

- Provide guidance for implementing state-level policy (such as exit criteria) within the local context.

- Set policy for promotion of and grading practices for English language learners based on levels of language proficiency.

Planning Between ESL Program and Curriculum Coordinators

- Align English language proficiency and academic content standards, and infuse them into the curriculum.

- Create model units of instruction that incorporate both sets of standards.

- Offer a unified curriculum to be implemented at the district level.

- Volunteer to deliver model lessons in mainstream classrooms.

To effectively implement the English language proficiency standards, teachers and administrators need to work together toward the unified goal of improving the educational access, opportunities, understanding, and performance of English language learners. The current standards-based movement is comprehensive. Its ultimate success is contingent on the collaboration of educators at the classroom, school, and district levels. The preK–12 English language proficiency standards contribute to the ongoing educational reform efforts that affect English language learners in today's schools.

Glossary

Glossary

academic content standards: statements that define what students are expected to know and be able to do in order to attain competency in challenging subject matter associated with schooling

academic language: language used in the learning of academic content in formal schooling contexts; aspects of language strongly associated with literacy and academic achievement, including specialized academic terms or technical language, speech registers, and discourse related to each field of study

affective factors: influences that affect language learning, such as emotions, self-esteem, investment, resilience, empathy, anxiety, attitude, and motivation

alignment: the extent of match among standards, assessment, curriculum, and instruction

benchmark grade level: the highest grade level within a grade-level cluster (For the English language proficiency standards, the benchmark grade levels are K, 3, 5, 8, and 12.)

biculturalism: the ability to negotiate effectively within two different cultural systems

bilingualism: the use of two languages by the same person or group

communicative competence: the ability to recognize and produce authentic and appropriate language correctly and fluently in any situation; the use of language in realistic, everyday settings; involves grammatical competence, sociolinguistic competence, discourse competence, and strategic competence

content-based instruction: also called *content-based English as a second language;* a model of language education that integrates language and content instruction in the classroom; an approach to second language learning in which second language teachers use instructional materials, learning tasks, and classroom techniques from academic content areas as the vehicle for developing second language, content, cognitive, and study skills

core content areas: specific curriculum subject matter areas, namely, English language arts, mathematics, science, and social studies

cross-cultural competence: the ability to function according to the cultural rules of more than one cultural system; the ability to respond in culturally sensitive and appropriate ways according to the cultural demands of a given situation (also called intercultural competence)

culture: the sum total of the ways of life of a people, including norms, learned behavior patterns, attitudes, and artifacts; also involves traditions, habits, or customs; how people behave, feel, and interact; the means by which they order and interpret the world; ways of perceiving, relating, and interpreting events based on established social norms; a system of standards for perceiving, believing, evaluating, and acting

discourse: language in context across all forms and modes; a term used to describe relatively large chunks of conversation or connected written text

ELL: English language learner; refers to a nonnative English speaker who is acquiring English; in contrast to other terms (e.g., limited English proficient), this term focuses on what students can do

ESL: the field of English as a second language; curriculum, courses, classes, and/or programs designed for students learning English as an additional language

general vocabulary: terms not directly associated with a specific content area (e.g., *summarize, book*)

grade-level clusters: grade spans for the English language proficiency standards (In this volume, five grade-level clusters are used: preK–K, 1–3, 4–5, 6–8, and 9–12.)

high-frequency vocabulary: terms used regularly in everyday situations (e.g., *open, school*)

home language: language(s) spoken in the home by significant others (e.g., family members, caregivers) who reside in the home; sometimes used as a synonym for *first language, primary language, native language,* or *heritage language*

instructional language: a special variety of language used in classrooms and governed by the different roles that teachers and students assume and the kinds of activities that occur

intercultural competence: the ability to function according to the cultural rules of more than one cultural system; the ability to respond in culturally sensitive and appropriate ways according to the cultural demands of a given situation (also called *cross-cultural competence*)

L1: first or native language

L2: second language, generally English

language domains: also called language *modes* or *skills*; each of the four broad categories (listening, speaking, reading, and writing) in which language is arbitrarily divided to assist with planning and delivery of instruction and assessment

language function: how language is used in the communication of a message

language proficiency: the level of competence at which an individual is able to use language for both basic communicative tasks and academic purposes

language proficiency levels: the demarcations along the second language acquisition continuum that are defined within the standards by a series of sample performance indicators

lexicon: vocabulary or corpus of language composed of words, phrases, and expressions

linguistic competence: a broad term used to describe the totality of a given individual's language ability; the underlying language system believed to exist as inferred from an individual's language performance

linguistic complexity: the degree of difficulty in oral or written discourse as determined by the syntactic and morphological structures and by the density or amount of information included

listening: the domain of language proficiency that encompasses how students process, understand, interpret, and respond to spoken language for a variety of purposes and in a variety of situations

metacognitive awareness: the knowledge of a range of problem-solving strategies, such as planning and goal setting, regarded as the key to successful language learning

metalinguistic awareness: the process of thinking about and reflecting on the structural features of spoken language, such as phonemes, words, sentences, and propositions

multiculturalism: the dynamic and complex coexistence of diverse cultures in a society or country

native culture: the culture that a person acquires first in life or identifies with as a member of a group

native language: primary or first language spoken by an individual

performance definitions: statements that indicate the extent to which students are meeting the stated standards; in the case of English language proficiency standards, performance definitions correspond to descriptions of what students can do at each language proficiency level

performance standards: statements that refer to how well students are meeting a content standard; specify the quality and effect of student performance at various levels of competency (benchmarks); statements of how students demonstrate their proficiency and progress toward meeting a standard

pragmatics: a subfield of linguistics; the study of natural language understanding, and specifically the study of how context influences the interpretation of meanings

primary language: first or native language spoken by an individual

productive language: refers to the language domains of speaking and writing

proficiency: the ability to function competently in the native or second language, involving a sense for appropriate linguistic behavior in a variety of situations

reading: the domain of language proficiency that encompasses how students process, interpret, and evaluate written language, symbols, and text with understanding and fluency

realia: authentic objects used to relate classroom teaching to real life (e.g., use of actual foods and supermarket circulars to develop the language related to foods or food purchasing)

receptive language: refers to the language domains of listening and reading

register: usage of different varieties of language, depending on the setting, the relationship among the individuals involved in the communication, and the function of the interaction; a form of a language that is appropriate to the social or functional context

sample performance indicators (SPIs): illustrative language behaviors associated with each language proficiency level; examples of assessable tasks that students can be expected to know or do as they approach the transition to the next level of English language proficiency in any given standard

scaffolding: providing support during instruction via instructional strategies (e.g., modeling, feedback, questioning techniques), contextual support (e.g., pictures, diagrams, lists), or classroom arrangements and processes (e.g., working in groups, pairs, activating previous knowledge); using one level of language proficiency as the foundation for building the next level

sheltered instruction: an approach in which students develop knowledge in specific content areas through the medium of English, their second language; teachers adjust the language demands of the lesson in many ways, such as modifying speech rate and tone, using context clues and models extensively, relating instruction to student experience, adapting the language of texts or tasks, and using certain methods familiar to language teachers (e.g., demonstrations, visuals, graphic organizers, cooperative work) to make academic instruction more accessible to students of different English proficiency levels

social language: the aspects of language proficiency strongly associated with basic fluency in face-to-face interaction; natural speech in social interactions, including those that occur in a classroom

sociocultural competence: the ability to function effectively in a particular social or cultural context according to the rules or expectancies for behavior held by members of that social or cultural group

sociolinguistic competence: related to communicative competence; the extent to which language is appropriately understood and used in a given situation (e.g., ability to make apologies, give compliments, politely refuse requests)

speaking: the domain of language proficiency that encompasses how students engage in oral communication in a variety of situations for a variety of purposes and audiences

specialized vocabulary: terms associated with a particular content area (e.g., *hypotheses* in science, *measures of central tendency* in mathematics)

standards: relatively stable criteria used to judge persons, institutions, programs, performance, and/or other outcomes; statements that describe the attainment, excellence, or requirement for desired behavior or practice; knowledge and skills that a learner or teacher should possess to perform well

strand: the series of sample performance indicators across language proficiency levels within a language domain and grade cluster

strategy: an individual instructional activity as it occurs in the classroom with built-in support for English language learners

support: a scaffold to assist learners with the communication act and facilitate their access to content (e.g., communicating with a partner, using graphic organizers)

syntax: the sentence structure or grammatical strings of a language

technical vocabulary: terms associated with a specific content-area topic (e.g., *Pythagorean theorem, government energy conservation project*)

transformation of sample performance indicators: a process for helping educators adapt sample performance indicators to design instruction that suits individual classrooms and student needs; entails changing one or more of the elements making up a sample performance indicator—language function, content, or support/strategy—to reflect local instructional targets

writing: the domain of language proficiency that encompasses how students engage in written communication in a variety of forms for a variety of purposes

Source Documents
and References for
Further Reading

Source Documents and References for Further Reading

Source Documents

No Child Left Behind Act of 2001, Pub. L. No. 107-110, 115 Stat. 1425 (2001). Retrieved January 13, 2006, from http://www.ed.gov/nclb/landing.jhtml?src=pb
This act is the latest reauthorization of the federal Elementary and Secondary Education Act enacted in 1965 to provide support and funding to K–12 schools in the United States.

WIDA Consortium. (2004). *English language proficiency standards for English language learners in kindergarten through Grade 12.* Madison: Wisconsin Department of Public Instruction. Retrieved January 13, 2006, from http://www.wida.us/
The World-Class Instructional Design and Assessment (WIDA) Consortium is a group of states that has developed English language proficiency standards for K–12 English language learners; its framework is the basis for the preK–12 English language proficiency standards in this volume.

Standards and Curriculum Documents by State

Arkansas

Arkansas Department of Education. (1999a). *Mathematics curriculum framework.* Little Rock: Author.

Arkansas Department of Education. (1999b). *Science curriculum framework.* Little Rock: Author.

Arkansas Department of Education. (2002). *English language acquisition framework.* Little Rock: Author.

California

California Department of Education. (2005). *Guiding principles: First class: A guide for early primary education.* Sacramento, CA: Author. Retrieved January 3, 2006, from http://www.cde.ca.gov/ci/gs/em/frstclsprinciples.asp

California State Board of Education. (2004). *Content standards.* Sacramento, CA: Author. Retrieved January 3, 2006, from http://www.cde.ca.gov/be/st/ss/

Delaware

Department of Public Instruction. (1995a). *New directions for education in Delaware: English language arts curriculum framework.* Dover, DE: Author.

Department of Public Instruction. (1995b). *New directions for education in Delaware: Mathematics curriculum framework.* Dover, DE: Author.

District of Columbia

District of Columbia Public Schools. (1999). *Benchmark document.* Washington, DC: Author.

District of Columbia Public Schools. (2002a). *Curriculum at a glance: Grades pre-kindergarten–12th grade.* Washington, DC: Author.

District of Columbia Public Schools. (2002b). *The portfolio and NEP/LEP matrix assessment procedures.* Washington, DC: Author.

Florida

Florida Department of Education. (2003). *Sunshine state standards.* Tallahassee, FL: Author. Retrieved January 3, 2006, from http://www.firn.edu/doe/curric/prek12/frame2.htm

Illinois

City of Chicago Board of Education. (1999). *Chicago Public Schools English as a second language goals and standards for pre-K through 12.* Chicago: Author.

Illinois State Board of Education. (1997). *Illinois learning standards.* Springfield, IL: Author.

Illinois State Board of Education, Division of Early Childhood Education. (2000). *Illinois early learning standards.* Springfield, IL: Author.

Illinois State Board of Education. (2003). *Assessment frameworks: Mathematics (grades 3–8), reading (grades 3–8), science (grades 4 and 7), and social science (grades 5 and 8).* Springfield, IL: Author.

Maine

Maine Department of Education. (1997). *State of Maine: Learning results.* Augusta, ME: Author.

New Jersey

New Jersey Department of Education. (2004). *Academic and professional standards: Curriculum and instruction.* Trenton, NJ: Author. Retrieved January 3, 2006, from http://www.nj.gov/njded/aps/cccs/

New York

New York State Academy for Teaching and Learning. (n.d.). *New York State learning standards.* Albany: New York State Education Department. Retrieved January 3, 2006, from http://www.emsc.nysed.gov /nysatl/standards.html

Pennsylvania

Pennsylvania Department of Education. (2005). *Language proficiency standards for English language learners: PreK–12.* Harrisburg, PA: Author. Retrieved April 25, 2006, from http://www.pde.state.pa.us /esl/cwp/view.asp?a=3&Q=110015&eslNav=|6449|&eslNav=|6449|

Pennsylvania Department of Education and Department of Public Welfare. (2005). *Pennsylvania early learning standards.* Harrisburg, PA: Author. Retrieved January 3, 2006, from http://www.pde.state .pa.us/early_childhood/lib/earlychildhood/EarlyLearningStandardsMarch_05.pdf

Rhode Island

Rhode Island Department of Elementary and Secondary Education. (1995). *Mathematical power for ALL students: The Rhode Island mathematics framework K–12.* Providence, RI: Author.

Rhode Island Department of Elementary and Secondary Education. (1996). *Literacy for ALL students: The Rhode Island English language arts framework.* Providence, RI: Author.

Texas

Texas Education Agency. (1999). *Texas prekindergarten curriculum guidelines.* Austin, TX: Author. Retrieved January 3, 2006, from http://www.tea.state.tx.us/curriculum/early/prekguide.pdf

Texas Education Agency. (2003). *Texas essential knowledge and skills (TEKS).* Austin, TX: Author. Retrieved January 3, 2006, from http://www.tea.state.tx.us/teks/index.html

Vermont

Vermont Department of Education. (2002). *Vermont's framework of standards and learning opportunities.* Montpelier, VT: Author.

Wisconsin

Wisconsin Department of Public Instruction. (2002). *Alternate performance indicators (APIs) for limited English proficient students.* Madison, WI: Author. Retrieved January 3, 2006, from http://www.dpi.state .wi.us/dpi/dlsea/equity/biling.html

Professional Organizations

English as a Second Language

National Study of School Evaluation. (2002). *Program evaluation: English as a second language.* Schaumburg, IL: Author.

TESOL. (1997). *ESL standards for pre-K–12 students.* Alexandria, VA: Author.

Language Arts

National Council of Teachers of English & International Reading Association. (2004). *Standards for the English language arts.* Urbana, IL: National Council of Teachers of English. Retrieved January 3, 2006, from http://www.ncte.org/about/over/standards/110846.htm

Mathematics

National Council of Teachers of Mathematics. (2004). Principles and standards for school mathematics. Reston, VA: Author. Retrieved January 3, 2006, from http://standards.nctm.org/

Science

National Science Teachers Association. (1996). *National science education standards.* Arlington, VA: Author. Retrieved January 3, 2006, from http://www.nsta.org/standards/

Social Studies

National Council for the Social Studies. (1994). *Expectations of excellence: Curriculum standards for the social studies.* Silver Spring, MD: Author. Retrieved January 3, 2006, from http://www.socialstudies .org/standards/

Further Reading

Standards-Based Education

Agor, B. (2001). (Ed.). (2001). *Integrating the ESL standards into classroom practice: Grades 9–12.* Alexandria, VA: TESOL.

American Council for the Teaching of Foreign Languages. (1986). *ACTFL proficiency guidelines.* Hastings-on-Hudson, NY: Author.

American Educational Research Association & American Psychological Association. (1999). *Standards for educational and psychological testing.* Washington, DC: American Psychological Association.

Council of Europe. (2001). *Common European framework of reference for languages: Learning, teaching, assessment.* Cambridge: Cambridge University Press.

Gottlieb, M. (2004). *WIDA Consortium English language proficiency standards for English language learners in Kindergarten through grade 12: Overview document.* Madison: State of Wisconsin.

Irujo, S. (Ed.). (2001). *Integrating the ESL standards into classroom practice: Grades 6–8.* Alexandria, VA: TESOL.

Kendall, J. S., & Marzano, R. J. (1997). *Content knowledge: A compendium of standards and benchmarks for K–12 education* (2nd ed.). Alexandria, VA: Association for Supervision & Curriculum Development.

Kuhlman, N., & Nadeau, A. (1999). English language development standards: The California model. *CATESOL Journal, 11*(1), 143–160.

McKeon, D. (1994). When meeting "common" standards is uncommonly difficult. *Educational Leadership, 51*(8), 45–49.

Morrow, K. (2004). *Insights from the Common European Framework.* Oxford: Oxford University Press.

Neill, M., Guisbond, L., & Schaeffer, B. (2004). *Failing our children: How "No Child Left Behind" undermines quality and equity in education: An accountability model that supports school improvement.* Cambridge, MA: FairTest.

Sacks, P. (1999). *Standardized minds: The high price of America's testing culture and what we can do to change it.* New York: Perseus Books.

Samway, K. D. (Ed.). (2001). *Integrating the ESL standards into classroom practice: Grades 3–5.* Alexandria, VA: TESOL.

Short, D. J., Gómez, E. L., Cloud, N., Katz, A., Gottlieb, M., & Malone, M., with Hamayan, E., Hudelson, S., & Ramírez, J. (2002). *Training others to use the ESL standards: A professional development manual.* Alexandria, VA: TESOL.

Smallwood, B. A. (Ed.). (2001). *Integrating the ESL standards into classroom practice: Grades pre-K–2.* Alexandria, VA: TESOL.

Snow, M. A. (Ed.). (2000). *Implementing the ESL standards for pre-K–12 students through teacher education.* Alexandria, VA: TESOL.

TESOL. (1997). *ESL standards for pre-K–12 students.* Alexandria, VA: Author.

TESOL. (1998). *Managing the assessment process: A framework for measuring student attainment of the ESL standards* (TESOL Professional Papers No. 5). Alexandria, VA: Author.

TESOL. (2001). *Scenarios for ESL standards-based assessment*. Alexandria, VA: Author.

Trumbull, E., & Farr, B. (Eds.). (2000). *Grading and reporting student progress in an age of standards*. Norwood, MA: Christopher-Gordon.

Bilingualism, Multiculturalism, and Cultural Competence

August, D., & Hakuta, K. (Eds.). (1998). *Educating language minority children*. Washington, DC: National Academy Press.

Baker, C. (2001). *Foundations of bilingual education and bilingualism* (3rd ed.). Clevedon, England: Multilingual Matters.

Banks, J. A., & Banks, C. A. M. (2004). *Handbook of research on multicultural education* (2nd ed.). San Francisco, CA: Jossey-Bass.

Bialystok, E., & Hakuta, K. (1994). *In other words: The science and psychology of second-language acquisition*. New York: Basic Books.

Carrasquillo, A. L., & Rodriguez, V. (2002). *Language minority students in the mainstream classroom* (2nd ed.). Tonawanda, NY: Multilingual Matters.

Christian, D., & Genesee, F. (Eds.). (2001). *Bilingual education* (Case Studies in TESOL Practice Series). Alexandria, VA: TESOL.

Cloud, N., Genesee, F., & Hamayan, E. (2000). *Dual language instruction: A handbook for enriched education*. Boston: Heinle & Heinle.

Cummins, J. (1981). The role of primary language development in promoting educational success for language minority students. In California State Department of Education, *Schooling and language minority students: A theoretical framework* (pp. 3–49). Los Angeles: California State University, Evaluation, Dissemination, & Assessment Center.

Cummins, J. (2000). *Language, power, and pedagogy: Bilingual children in the crossfire*. Clevedon, England: Multilingual Matters.

Faltis, C. J., & Hudelson, S. J. (1998). *Bilingual education in elementary and secondary school communities: Toward understanding and caring*. Needham Heights, MA: Allyn & Bacon.

Genesee, F. (Ed.). (1994). *Educating second language children*. New York: Cambridge University Press.

Hornberger, N. H. (Ed.). (2003). *Continua of biliteracy: An ecological framework for educational policy, research, and practice in multilingual settings*. Clevedon, England: Multilingual Matters.

Hymes, D. H. (1972). On communicative competence. In J. B. Pride & J. Holmes (Eds.), *Sociolinguistics* (pp. 269–293). Harmondsworth, England: Penguin Books.

Larsen-Freeman, D., & Long, M. H. (1991). *An introduction to second language acquisition research*. New York: Longman.

Lessow-Hurley, J. (2005). *The foundations of dual language instruction* (4th ed.). New York: Longman.

Lucas, T., & Katz, A. (1994). Reframing the debate: The roles of native languages in English-only programs for language minority students. *TESOL Quarterly, 28,* 537–562.

McKay, S., & Hornberger, N. H. (Eds.). (1996). *Sociolinguistics and language teaching*. New York: Cambridge University Press.

Minami, M., & Ovando, C. J. (2004). Language issues in multicultural contexts. In J. A. Banks & C. A. M. Banks (Eds.), *Handbook of research on multicultural education* (2nd ed., pp. 427–444). San Francisco, CA: Jossey-Bass.

Miramontes, O. B., Nadeau, A., & Commins, N. L. (1997). *Restructuring schools for linguistic diversity*. New York: Teachers College Press.

Nieto, S. (2004). *Affirming diversity: The sociopolitical context for multicultural education* (4th ed.). White Plains, NY: Longman.

Ovando, C. J., Combs, M. C., & Collier, C. P. (2006). *Bilingual and ESL classrooms: Teaching in multicultural contexts* (4th ed.). New York: McGraw-Hill.

Snow, M. A. (2005). Primary language instruction: A bridge to English language development. In California State Department of Education, *Schooling and language minority students: A theoretico-practical framework* (3rd ed., pp. 119–160). Los Angeles: California State University, Evaluation, Dissemination, & Assessment Center.

Thomas, W. P., & Collier, V. P. (2002). *A national study of school effectiveness for language minority students' long-term academic achievement*. Santa Cruz, CA: University of California, Center for Research on Education, Diversity & Excellence.

Academic Language Proficiency

Anderson, N. J. (2005). L2 learning strategies. In E. Hinkel (Ed.), *Handbook of research in second language teaching and learning* (pp. 757–771). Mahwah, NJ: Lawrence Erlbaum.

Bailey, A. L., Butler, F. A., LaFramenta, C., & Ong, C. (2004). *Towards the characterization of academic language in upper elementary science classrooms* (CSE Report 621). Los Angeles: University of California, National Center for Research on Evaluation, Standards, & Student Testing.

Chamot, A. U. (2005). The cognitive academic language learning approach (CALLA): An update. In P. Richard-Amato & M. A. Snow (Eds.), *Academic success for English language learners* (pp. 87–101). White Plains, NY: Longman.

Cummins, J. (2005). Teaching the language of academic success: A framework for school-based language policies. In California State Department of Education, *Schooling and language minority students: A theoretico-practical framework* (3rd ed., pp. 3–32). Los Angeles: California State University, Evaluation, Dissemination, & Assessment Center.

Echevarria, J., Vogt, M. E., & Short, D. (2004). *Making content comprehensible for English Language Learners* (2nd ed.). Needham Heights, MA: Allyn & Bacon.

Freeman, Y. S., & Freeman, D. (2002). *Closing the achievement gap: How to reach limited-formal-schooling and long-term English learners*. Portsmouth, NH: Heinemann.

Goodman, Y. (2003). *Valuing language study: Inquiry into language for elementary and middle schools*. Urbana, IL: National Council of Teachers of English.

Nation, I. S. P. (2001). *Learning vocabulary in another language*. Cambridge: Cambridge University Press.

Richard-Amato, P., & Snow, M. A. (2005). *Academic success for English language learners: Strategies for K–12 mainstream teachers*. White Plains, NY: Longman.

Scarcella, R. (2003a). *Academic English: A conceptual framework* (Technical Report 2003-1). Irvine: University of California, Linguistic Minority Research Institute.

Scarcella, R. (2003b). *Accelerating academic English: A focus on English language learners*. Oakland: Regents of the University of California.

Schleppegrell, M. J. (2004). *The language of schooling: A functional linguistics perspective*. Mahwah, NJ: Lawrence Erlbaum.

Literacy and Oral Language Development of English Language Learners

Bauman, J. F., Kame'enui, E. J., & Ash, G. E. (2002). Research on vocabulary instruction: Voltaire redux. In J. Flood, D. Lapp, D. R. Squire, & J. Jensen (Eds.), *Handbook of research on the teaching of English language arts* (pp. 752–785). Mahwah, NJ: Lawrence Erlbaum.

Christensen, L. (2000). *Reading, writing, and rising up*. Milwaukee, WI: Rethinking Schools.

Dutro, S., & Moran, C. (2003). Rethinking English language instruction: An architectural approach. In G. Garcia (Ed.), *English learners: Reaching the highest level of English literacy* (pp. 227–258). Newark, DE: International Reading Association.

Enright, D. S., & McCloskey, M. L. (1988). *Integrating English: Developing English language and literacy in the multilingual classroom*. Reading, MA: Addison-Wesley.

Ernst, G. (1994). Talking circle: Conversation and negotiation in the ESL classroom. *TESOL Quarterly, 28,* 293–322.

Ernst-Slavit, G., & Mulhern, M. (2003, September/October). Bilingual books: Promoting literacy and biliteracy in the second-language and mainstream classroom. *Reading Online, 7*(2). Retrieved January 3, 2006, from http://www.readingonline.org/articles/art_index.asp?HREF=ernst-slavit/index.html

Freeman, Y. S., & Freeman, D. (2000). *Teaching reading in multicultural classrooms*. Portsmouth, NH: Heinemann.

Goodman, K. S. (1982a). *Language and literacy: The selected writings of Kenneth S. Goodman: Vol. 1. Process, theory, research* (F. V. Gollasch, Ed.). Boston: Routledge & Kegan Paul.

Goodman, K. S. (1982b). *Language and literacy: The selected writings of Kenneth S. Goodman: Vol. 2. Reading, language and the classroom teacher* (F. V. Gollasch, Ed.). Boston: Routledge & Kegan Paul.

Green, J., & Dixon, C. (1993). Introduction: Talking knowledge into being: Discursive and social practices in classrooms. *Linguistics and Education, 5*(3&4), 231–239.

Hawkins, M. R. (2004). Researching English language and literacy development in schools. *Educational Researcher 33*(3), 14–25.

Hill, B. C. (2001). *Developmental continuums: A framework for literacy instruction and assessment K–8*. Norwood, MA: Christopher-Gordon.

Kucer, S. B. (2005). *Dimensions of literacy: A conceptual base for teaching reading and writing in school settings* (2nd ed.). Mahwah, NJ: Lawrence Erlbaum.

Kucer, S. B., & Silva, C. (2006). *Teaching the dimensions of literacy*. Mahwah, NJ: Lawrence Erlbaum.

Nation, I. S. P. (2001). *Learning vocabulary in another language*. Cambridge: Cambridge University Press.

Pardo, E. B., & Tinajero, J. V. (1993). Literacy instruction through Spanish: Linguistic, cultural, and pedagogical considerations. In J. Tinajero & A. F. Ada (Eds.), *The power of two languages: Literacy and biliteracy for Spanish-speaking students* (pp. 26–36). New York: Macmillan/McGraw-Hill.

Peregoy, S., & Boyle, O. (2005). *Reading, writing, and learning in ESL: A resource book for teachers* (4th ed.). Boston: Pearson.

Slavin, R. E., & Cheung, A. (2003). *Effective reading programs for English language learners: A best-evidence synthesis* (Report No. 66). Baltimore, MD: John Hopkins University, Center for Research on the Education of Students Placed at Risk.

Slavin, R. E., & Cheung, A. (2004). How do English language learners learn to read? *Educational Leadership, 61*(6), 52–57.

Snow, M. A. (2005). A model of academic literacy for integrated language and content instruction. In E. Hinkel (Ed.), *Handbook of research in second language teaching and learning* (pp. 693–712). Mahwah, NJ: Lawrence Erlbaum.

Tinajero, J. V., & Ada, A. F. (Eds.). (1993). *The power of two languages: Literacy and biliteracy for Spanish-speaking students.* New York: Macmillan/McGraw-Hill.

Vacca, R., & Vacca, J. (1999). *Content area reading.* New York: Longman.

Content-Based Instruction

Adamson, H. D. (1993). *Academic competence: Theory and classroom practice: Preparing ESL students for content courses.* New York: Longman.

Chamot, A. U., & O'Malley, J. M. (1994). *The CALLA handbook: Implementing the cognitive academic language learning approach.* New York: Addison-Wesley.

Echevarria, J., Short, D. J., & Vogt, M. E. (2004). *Making content comprehensible for English language learners: The SIOP model* (2nd ed.). Boston: Allyn & Bacon.

Ernst-Slavit, G., Moore, M., & Maloney, C. (2002). Changing lives: Teaching English and literature to ESL students. *Journal of Adolescent and Adult Literacy, 48*(2), 116–128.

Faltis, C. (1997). *Joinfostering: Adapting teaching for the multilingual classroom* (2nd ed.). Upper Saddle River, NJ: Merrill.

Fathman, A. K., & Crowther, D. T. (2006). (Eds.). *Science for English language learners: K–12 classroom strategies.* Arlington, VA: National Science Teachers Association Press.

Kaufman, D., & Crandall, J. (Eds.). (2005). *Content-based instruction in primary and secondary school settings.* Alexandria, VA: TESOL.

Mohan, B. (1986). *Language and content.* Reading, MA: Addison-Wesley.

Reiss, J. (2001). *ESOL strategies for teaching content: Facilitating instruction for English language learners.* Upper Saddle River, NJ: Prentice Hall.

Reiss, J. (2005). *Teaching content to English language learners.* White Plains, NY: Pearson Longman.

Richard-Amato, P. A. (2003). *Making it happen: From interactive to participatory language teaching* (3rd ed.). White Plains, NY: Pearson Education.

Short, D. J. (1994a). The challenge of social studies for limited English proficient students. *Social Education, 58*(1), 36–38.

Short, D. J. (1994b). Expanding middle school horizons: Integrating language, culture, and social studies. *TESOL Quarterly, 28*, 581–608.

Short, D. J. (2002). Language and learning in sheltered social studies classes. *TESOL Journal, 11*(1), 18–24.

Snow, M. A., & Brinton, D. M. (Eds.). (1997). *The content-based classroom: Perspectives on integrating language and content*. White Plains, NY: Addison-Wesley.

Assessment of English Language Learners

Aisworth, L., & Christinson, J. (1998). *Student generated rubrics: An assessment model to help all students succeed*. Orangeburg, NY: Dale Seymour.

Alderson, J. C. (2000). *Assessing reading*. Cambridge: Cambridge University Press.

Arter, J., & McTighe, J. (2001). *Scoring rubrics in the classroom: Using performance criteria for assessing and improving student performance*. Thousand Oaks, CA: Corwin Press.

Bachman, L. F., & Palmer, A. S. (1996). *Fundamental considerations in language testing*. Oxford: Oxford University Press.

Brown, H. D. (2004). *Language assessment: Principles and classroom practices*. White Plains, NY: Pearson.

Buck, G. (2001). *Assessing listening*. Cambridge: Cambridge University Press.

Butler, F. A., & Stevens, R. (2001). Standardized assessment of the content knowledge of English language learners K–12: Current trends and old dilemmas. *Language Testing, 18*, 409–428.

Coltrane, B. (2002, November). *English language learners and high stakes tests: An overview of the issues* (ERIC Digest EDO-FL-02-07) [Electronic version]. Washington, DC: ERIC Clearinghouse on Languages & Linguistics. Retrieved January 3, 2006, from http://www.cal.org/ericcll/digest/0207coltrane.html

Darian, S. (2003). *Understanding the language of science*. Austin: University of Texas Press.

Farr, B. P., & Trumbull, E. (1997). *Assessment alternatives for diverse classrooms*. Norwood, MA: Christopher-Gordon.

Fradd, S. H., & McGee, P. L. (1994). *Instructional assessment: An integrated approach to evaluating student performance*. Reading, MA: Addison-Wesley.

Genesee, F., & Upshur, J. A. (1996). *Classroom-based evaluation in second language education*. Cambridge: Cambridge University Press.

Glatthorn, A. A. (1998). *Performance assessment and standards-based curricula: The achievement cycle*. Larchmont, NY: Eye on Education.

Gottlieb, M. (1995). Nurturing student learning through portfolios. *TESOL Journal, 5*(1), 12–14.

Gottlieb, M. (2000). Standards-based, large-scale assessment. In M. A. Snow (Ed.), *Implementing the ESL standards for Pre-K–12 students through teacher education* (pp. 167–186). Alexandria, VA: TESOL.

Gottlieb, M. (2003). *Large-scale assessment of English language learners: Addressing accountability in K–12 settings* (TESOL Professional Papers No. 6). Alexandria, VA: TESOL.

Gottlieb, M. (2006). *Assessing English language learners: Bridges from language proficiency to academic achievement*. Thousand Oaks, CA: Corwin Press.

Gottlieb, M., & Boals, T. (2005). On the road to MECCA: Assessing content-based instruction within a standards framework. In D. Kaufman & J. Crandall (Eds.), *Content-based instruction in primary and secondary school settings* (pp. 145–161). Alexandria, VA: TESOL.

Grissom, J. B. (2004). Reclassification of English learners. *Education Policy Analysis Archives 12*(36), 1–36.

Guskey, T. R., & Bailey, J. M. (2001). *Developing grading and reporting systems for student learning.* Thousand Oaks, CA: Corwin Press.

Katz, A. (2000). Changing paradigms for assessment. In M. A. Snow (Ed.), *Implementing the ESL standards for Pre-K–12 students through teacher education* (pp. 137–166). Alexandria, VA: TESOL.

LaCelle-Peterson, M. W., & Rivera, C. (1994). Is it real for all kids? A framework for equitable assessment policies for English language learners. *Harvard Educational Review, 64*(1), 55–75.

Murphy, S., & Underwood, T. (2000). *Portfolio practices: Lessons from schools, districts, and states.* Norwood, MA: Christopher-Gordon.

North, B. (2000). *The development of a common framework scale of language proficiency.* New York: Peter Lang.

O'Malley, J. M., & Pierce, L. V. (1996). *Authentic assessment for English language learners: Practical approaches for teachers.* New York: Addison-Wesley.

Salvia, J., & Ysseldyke, J. E. (2004). *Assessment in special and inclusive education.* Boston: Houghton Mifflin.

Shohamy, E. (2001). *The power of tests: A critical perspective on the uses of language tests.* London,: Pearson Education.

Short, D. (1993). Assessing integrated language and content instruction. *TESOL Quarterly, 27,* 627–656.

Smith, J. K., Smith, L. F., & De Lisi, R. (2001). *Natural classroom assessment: Designing seamless instruction and assessment.* Thousand Oaks, CA: Corwin Press.

TESOL. (2000, June). Assessment and accountability of English for speakers of other languages (ESOL) students [Policy statement]. Retrieved January 3, 2006, from http://www.tesol.org/s_tesol/sec_document.asp?CID=32&DID=369

Valdez Pierce, L. (2001). Assessment of reading comprehension strategies for intermediate bilingual students. In S. J. Hurley & J. V. Tinajero (Eds.), *Literacy assessment of second language learners* (pp. 64–83). Boston: Allyn & Bacon.

Valdez Pierce, L. (2003). *Assessing English language learners.* Washington, DC: National Education Association.

Appendixes

Appendix A:
Frequently Asked Questions
About the PreK–12 English Language
Proficiency Standards

Why did TESOL create preK–12 English language proficiency standards?

TESOL wanted to bring its ESL standards up to date so that they would reflect current theory and research, emphasize content-based instructional practice, and address the requirements of the No Child Left Behind (NCLB) Act of 2001.

What did TESOL use as the starting point in developing the preK–12 English language proficiency standards?

When TESOL began to consider revising the ESL standards in 2003, the framework developed by the World-Class Instructional Design and Assessment (WIDA) Consortium of states offered the most comprehensive document addressing academic proficiency in content areas for English language learners. Other foundational documents included TESOL's (1997) preK–12 ESL standards, content standards from national organizations, and state standards frameworks.

Why did TESOL opt for five grade-level clusters?

The grade-level clusters (preK–K, 1–3, 4–5, 6–8, and 9–12) mirror current trends in instructional practices and typical grade-level divisions in preK–12 settings.

Why are there five language proficiency levels?

The five levels (Starting, Emerging, Developing, Expanding, and Bridging) reflect a continuum that captures the complexity of the second language development process. The performance definitions provide specific descriptions of the stages of language acquisition for use in instruction and assessment.

Which academic content standards are addressed?

TESOL selected the core academic content areas (language arts, math, science, and social studies) in addition to the ESL standards in response to curricular foci and federal legislation, and in accordance with the framework of the WIDA Consortium. The national standards for these content areas provided the overarching categories for the development process. The academic content standards from states with the largest population of English language learners were analyzed in conjunction with those from the states represented by WIDA. Together, more than 3 million of the 5 million English language learners nationwide reside in these states.

How do these standards meet the requirements of the No Child Left Behind Act?

By integrating language and content, the English language proficiency standards reflect the new emphasis on academic language proficiency that is anchored in state academic content standards. The standards are presented within four language domains and have descriptive levels of English language proficiency, as outlined in Titles I and III of NCLB.

How will this volume fit in with current state English language proficiency and academic content standards?

This standards framework is a model for states and districts to use in addressing the academic language demands English language learners face in school. Districts and states are welcome to adopt or adapt any of the ideas presented here to refine their own English language proficiency standards or to use TESOL's English language proficiency standards as a validity check against their own set of standards.

How are strategies incorporated into the English language proficiency standards?

Strategies are treated in two ways. First, for teachers, strategies are integrated into the sample performance indicators for English Language Proficiency Levels 1–4 in the form of visual, graphic, or interactional support. Second, for students, strategies are introduced through topics, such as in Standard 1, reading in grade-level clusters 4–5 and 9–12, and Standard 2, listening in grade-level cluster 4–5, and reading in grade-level cluster 6–8.

Appendix B:
The Alignment Process

Alignment is the degree of correspondence between two entities. The definition of alignment for this volume is more instructionally bound than other approaches (e.g., those concerned with the match between standards and assessments), as the overall purpose for English language proficiency standards is to support teachers and other educators in teaching the language of language arts, mathematics, science, and social studies with respect to the student's language proficiency level.

Here, we align the progress or performance indicators (of the ESL and language proficiency standards) with academic achievement standards (of academic content standards). Overall, a comprehensive survey and content analysis of standards of national organizations and states for language arts, mathematics, science, and social studies yielded common topics. Lists of these topics at the benchmark grades of each grade-level cluster (K, 3, 5, 8, and 12) were generated to use in developing the strands of sample performance indicators (see Appendix D).

Furthermore, the topics were matched against the content stems in the English language proficiency standards of TESOL, of the World-Class Instructional Design and Assessment (WIDA) Consortium, and of other states (see Source Documents and References for Further Reading). Here alignment reflects the degree of match of language functions at the varying levels of English language proficiency.

The following process was used to transform the performance indicators and achievement standards of national organizations, states, and the WIDA Consortium into those for TESOL's English language proficiency standards:

1. Create frameworks for analysis of the standards of each national organization.

2. Extract topics and develop a master list by benchmark grade levels (the highest grade level in the cluster) for each of the national standards.

3. Review academic content topics across state standards at benchmark grades and compared them to the master list.

4. Compare national and state topics with those within WIDA's strands of model performance indicators by domain.

5. Decide whether any topics not previously addressed should be developed into language proficiency strands (e.g., those present on both the national organizations' and the states' topic lists).

6. Assign a language domain to newly designated topics.

7. Develop a language proficiency strand for new topics, making sure the language function at the highest language proficiency level (Bridging) is comparable to that present in the academic content standards.

8. Infuse socially and culturally relevant strands and sample progress indicators from TESOL's 1997 volume into the language proficiency standards.

Appendix C:
Evidence of the Alignment
of the ESL Standards With the
English Language Proficiency Standards

The presentation of the English language proficiency standards is quite different from that of their predecessors, the ESL standards (TESOL, 1997), but much of the information from the sample descriptors and sample progress indicators has been retained in the sample performance indicators. Below are three examples of the connection between the two sets of standards. Evidence of this alignment in topics or levels of language proficiency is in boldface.

Example 1

ESL Standards (TESOL, 1997): Goal 1, Standard 1
To use English to communicate in social settings: Students will use English to participate in social interactions.
Grades: PreK–3
Sample progress indicator: **Describe feelings and emotions** (after watching a movie)

English Language Proficiency Standards: Standard 1
English language learners communicate for social, intercultural, and instructional purposes within the school setting.
Grade-level cluster: 1–3
Language domain: Speaking

Strand of sample performance indicators:

Topic	Level 1	Level 2	Level 3	Level 4	Level 5
Feelings **Emotions** Needs	Respond to everyday oral requests or questions from a partner	Make requests, ask questions, or state reactions to everyday events, situations, or cultural experiences with a partner	Describe or recount reactions to everyday events, situations, or cultural experiences in small groups	Elaborate, using details or examples, reactions to events, situations, or cultural experiences	Present skits reflecting reactions to events, situations, or cultural experiences

Example 2

ESL Standards (TESOL, 1997): Goal 3, Standard 3
To use English in socially and culturally appropriate ways: Students will use appropriate learning strategies to extend their sociolinguistic and sociocultural competence.
Grades: 4–8
Sample progress indicator: **Rephrase an utterance when it results in cultural misunderstanding**

English Language Proficiency Standards: Standard 1

English language learners communicate for social, intercultural, and instructional purposes within the school setting.
Grade-level cluster: 6–8
Language domain: Writing

Strand of sample performance indicators:

Topic	Level 1	Level 2	Level 3	Level 4	Level 5
Negotiating solutions to problems Interpersonal or **cultural misunderstandings**	Identify examples of common **cultural misunderstandings** among family and friends from videos or class discussions (in L1) with a partner	List examples of common **cultural misunderstandings** (e.g., chores or responsibilities) using visual or graphic support	Create descriptions or narrations of issues or **cultural misunderstandings** using visual or graphic support	Provide advice, **rephrase**, or offer possible solutions for **cultural misunderstandings** using visual models of writing (e.g., in newspapers)	Create guidelines for a group, class, or school on conflict resolution

Example 3

ESL Standards: Goal 2, Standard 2
To use English to achieve academically in all content areas: Students will use English to obtain, process, construct, and provide subject matter information in spoken and written form.
Grades: 9–12
Sample descriptor: Representing information visually and interpreting information presented visually

English Language Proficiency Standards: Standard 3
English language learners communicate information, ideas, and concepts necessary for academic success in the area of mathematics.
Grade-level cluster: 9–12
Language domain: Reading

Strand of sample performance indicators:

Topic	Level 1	Level 2	Level 3	Level 4	Level 5
Data displays Data interpretation	Match data in graphic representations from everyday sources (e.g., newspapers, magazines) to text with a partner	Sort and rank, with a partner, information gathered from data on graphs (e.g., stock quotes, sports statistics)	Analyze comparative language to draw conclusions from data in charts, tables, and graphs with a partner	**Organize, display, and interpret data** from **visually** or graphically supported material with a partner	Make predictions based on charts and graphs from modified grade-level text

Appendix D:
Content Topics Informing the English Language Proficiency Standards

These content topics were drawn from the national and state academic content standards listed in Source Documents and References for Further Reading. The topics are presented by content area and grade-level cluster with the exception of the ESL standards, which cover Grades K–12 and are categorized by goal. Many topics spiral and repeat over grade-level clusters; however, for the most part, they are listed when first introduced in national and state academic content standards.

Standards-Based Language Functions and Topics (PreK–12; TESOL, 1997)

Goal 1: To use English to communicate in social settings	Goal 2: To use English to achieve academically in all content areas	Goal 3: To use English in socially and culturally appropriate ways
<ul><li>Describe feelings and emotions</li><li>Defend and argue a position</li><li>Indicate interests, opinions, or preferences</li><li>Give and ask for permission</li><li>Offer and respond to greetings, compliments, invitations, introductions, and farewells</li><li>Negotiate solutions to problems, interpersonal misunderstandings, and disputes</li><li>Clarify and restate information</li><li>Write personal essays</li><li>Describe favorite storybook characters</li><li>Recount events of interest</li><li>Make recommendations</li><li>Use the primary language to ask for clarification</li><li>Associate realia or diagrams with written labels</li><li>Use written sources to discover or check information</li><li>Share social and cultural traditions and values</li><li>Use context to construct meaning</li><li>Self-monitor and self-evaluate language development</li></ul>	<ul><li>Compare and classify information</li><li>Synthesize, analyze, and evaluate information</li><li>Research information from multiple sources</li><li>Take a position and support it</li><li>Construct a chart</li><li>Identify and associate written symbols with words</li><li>Define, compare, and classify objects</li><li>Locate information</li><li>Edit and revise own written assignments</li><li>Use contextual clues</li><li>Consult print and nonprint resources in the native language</li><li>Write a summary</li><li>Record observations</li><li>Skim and scan materials</li><li>Rephrase, explain, revise, and expand information</li><li>Follow directions</li><li>Ask and answer questions</li><li>Express likes, dislikes, and needs</li><li>Explain actions</li><li>Gather and retell information</li><li>Represent information visually and interpret information presented visually</li><li>Connect new information to information previously learned</li></ul>	<ul><li>Recognize irony, sarcasm, and humor</li><li>Use idiomatic speech</li><li>Write business and personal letters</li><li>Write letters or e-mail messages using appropriate language forms</li><li>Compare body language norms among various cultures</li><li>Identify nonverbal cues that cause misunderstanding</li><li>Rephrase an utterance when it results in cultural misunderstanding</li><li>Respond to and use slang and idioms</li></ul>

Topics Drawn From National and State Academic Content Standards

Grade-Level Cluster	Academic Content Area			
	Language Arts and Reading	**Mathematics**	**Science**	**Social Studies**
PreK–K	**Genres** • Nursery rhymes • Chants and songs • Picture books • Fairy tales **Topics** • Environmental print • Concepts about print • Sounds and symbols	• Quantity • Patterns • Size • Spatial relations • Geometric shapes • Weight • Temperature • Measurement of time (calendar, clocks) • Numbers and operations	• Senses • Living things • Change in self and environment • Forces in nature • Seasons, night and day • Weather • Safety • Animals and habitats • Scientific process • Colors	• Community workers • Families • Location of objects and places • Transportation • Clothing • Food • Shelter • Holidays and symbols • Classroom, school • Neighborhood • Friends
1–3	**Genres** • Fiction • Nonfiction • Poetry • Predictable books • Folktales **Topics** • Sequence of story • Word families • Rhyming words • Homophones • Compound words • Story grammar • Phonics and phonemic awareness	• Time (digital and analog) • Measurement tools (standard, nonstandard, metric) • Place value • Money • Estimation • Capacity • Symmetry • Basic operations (addition and subtraction) • Whole numbers	• Light • Motion • Weathering and erosion • Renewable and nonrenewable resources • Plants • Animals • Life cycles • Living and nonliving things • Sound • Objects in the sky • Organisms and environment • Astronomy • Water cycle	• Needs of groups, societies, and cultures • Artifacts of the past • Representations of the earth (maps, globes, and photographs) • Land forms • Scale • Use of resources and land • Citizenship • Communities • Governments • Cultural heritage • Time and chronology

Grade-Level Cluster	Academic Content Area			
	Language Arts and Reading	**Mathematics**	**Science**	**Social Studies**
4–5	**Genres** • Biographies and autobiography • Fables • Fairy tales • Fantasy • Folklore • Informational texts • Legends • Mysteries • Myths • Narratives • Prose • Science fiction • Tall tales **Topics** • Affixes and root words • Fact and opinion • Hyperbole • Main ideas and details • Organization of texts • Phonemes and phonology • Point of view • Story grammar • Text structure and organization	• Angles • Area • Basic operations (multiplication and division) • Decimals • Descriptive statistics • Equivalent forms (fractions, decimals, and percent) • Fractions • Patterns and relationships • Percent • Perimeter • Polygons • Sets • Three-dimensional shapes • Data analysis • Patterns, relations, and functions	• Cells and organisms • Earth materials • Ecology and conservation • Ecosystems • Electricity • Energy sources • Forces of nature • Fossils • Geological forms • Heat • Magnetism • Reproduction and heredity • Scientific inquiry • Simple machines • Solar system • States of matter • Weather patterns • Types of resources • Body systems • Natural resources • Earth's history • Living systems	• Branches of government • Colonization • Communities • Explorers • Goods and services • Historical events, figures, and leaders • Immigration • Legends and scales • Maps and globes • Neighbors north and south • Prehistoric animals • Resources and products • Tools and artifacts • Topography • Trade routes • U.S. documents • U.S. regions: Rivers, coasts, mountains, deserts, and plains • Cross-cultural experiences

Grade-Level Cluster	Academic Content Area			
	Language Arts and Reading	**Mathematics**	**Science**	**Social Studies**
6–8	**Genres** • Adventure • Ballads • Editorials • Historical documents • Human interest • Multimedia • Mythology • Poetry and free verse • Science fiction • Technical texts **Topics** • Alliteration • Author's purpose • Dialogue • Metaphors and similes • Multiple meanings • Personification • Synonyms, antonyms, and homophones • Use of resources (including strategies and editing)	• Area, volume, and circumference • Complex two- and three-dimensional figures • Data sets and plots • Factors • Integers • Interpreting data and statistics • Line segments and angles • Measures of central tendency • Metric and U.S. customary units of measurement • Probability • Ratio and proportion • Square root • Statistics	• Atoms and molecules • Bacteria to plants • Body systems and organs • Chemical building blocks • Climate zones • Comets and meteorites • Elements and compounds • Forms of energy • Light • Motion and force • Natural disasters • Reproduction • Scientific invention • Solar system • Temperature changes • Water • Populations, resources, and environments	• Ancient and medieval civilizations • Bill of Rights • Civil War • Countries and continents • Forms and organization of government • Freedom and democracy • Longitude, latitude, and time zones • Revolution • Rights and responsibilities • Slavery • U.S. Constitution • Cultural perspectives and frames of reference

Grade-Level Cluster	Academic Content Area			
	Language Arts and Reading	**Mathematics**	**Science**	**Social Studies**
9–12	**Genres** • Critical commentary • Literary genres • Monologues • Research and Investigation • Autobiographical and biographical narratives **Topics** • Analogies • Author's perspective and point of view • Bias • Parody • Satire • Symbolism • Word derivations (etymology) • Literal and figurative language	• Data displays and interpretation • Derived attributes • Formulas and equations • Mathematical functions • Powers • Roots • Speed and acceleration • Angles • Quadrilaterals • Models • Scale and proportion • Congruence	• Atoms, molecules, and nuclear structures • Chemical and physical change • Compounds • Constellations • Food chains • Forces and motion • Genetics and heredity • Scientific research and investigation • Simple organisms • Taxonomic systems • Vertebrates and invertebrates • Conservation of energy and matter • Classification • Ecology and adaptation	• Global economy • Historical figures and times • Individual rights and responsibilities • Social issues and inequities • The story of the United States • World histories, civilizations, and cultures • Cultural diversity and cohesion • International and multinational organizations • Supreme Court cases • Federal, civil, and individual rights • Behaviors of individuals and groups • Production, consumption, and distribution • Supply and demand • Banking and money • Human populations